C000139581

Spirit Speaks

Spirit Speaks

QUESTIONS AND ANSWERS ON LIFE AND OUR SPIRIT CONNECTION

Shirley Battie

Copyright © 2010 by Shirley Battie.

Library of Congress Control Number: 2010903701
ISBN: Hardcover   978-1-4500-6111-7
               Softcover   978-1-4500-6110-0
               E-book   978-1-4500-6112-4

All rights reserved. No part of this book may be reproduced or transmitted in any form
or by any means, electronic or mechanical, including photocopying, recording, or by
any information storage and retrieval system, without permission in writing from the
copyright owner.

This book was printed in the United States of America.

Cover Design by Gwen Stace *gigi_stace@yahoo.co.uk*

To order additional copies of this book, contact:
Xlibris Corporation
0-800-644-6988
www.xlibrispublishing.co.uk
Orders@xlibrispublishing.co.uk
300221

CONTENTS

CHAPTER 3

CHAPTER 4

CHAPTER 5

CHAPTER 6

CHAPTER 7

CHAPTER 8

CHAPTER 9

OTHER WORLDS

CHAPTER 10

To my grown children who love me in spite of my not being like other moms and for letting me be who I am.
To my friends who have always had faith in me.

INTRODUCTION

This book is for readers who are just opening up to spirits and for those who have a lot of experience and for those in between. It ranges from basic understanding to higher awareness. Some of you will say "I already know all that." This just confirms how much you have grown and advanced. If that applies to you, then skip ahead to other subjects. I don't pretend to know all the answers and quite possibly have some wrong. They are meant to encourage debate and discussion. Apathy does not encourage change we may wish for. I know you are not apathetic, or you would not be reading this book.

What I currently explain and put forth in this book is always subject to change as understanding and knowledge expand. What I believe today may not be how I see things and believe in the future. Also what one doesn't understand today may be understood later on. I have answered the questions put to me as honestly and as accurately as I could.

These are some of the many questions exactly as they have been put to me by audiences at all levels of understanding during talks, channeling sessions, and correspondence. Some answers given have come directly from spirit during channeling sessions. There will be quotation marks (" ") when it is direct from spirit.

CHAPTER 1

METHODS OF SPIRIT COMMUNICATION

MEDIUMS, PSYCHICS, CLAIRVOYANTS, ETC.

Q. What is a medium?

A. A medium is a person who is used as a channel for something intangible to be passed through them. It has come to mean and is generally understood that a medium is one who can pass messages from the dearly departed to those still on earth. It goes much further than that however. There will be argument over that statement, but please take a look at my other explanations of the word *medium*. All individuals used as a means (channel) for passing through indefinable work can not only give messages from those in the fourth-dimensional world or higher but they also have other functions.

Various terms are used by the public such as, *clairvoyants, psychics*, and *fortune-tellers*—heaven forbid. Most mediums hate the term *fortune-tellers* since that they are not. The word *medium* covers a wide range of psychic and spiritual abilities. A man or woman can be used as a means of communication or transferring energies from higher vibrations into the conscious awareness. The content of what is brought through is using the medium, the means from which it comes, such as an incarnate person. Other terms for *medium* can be *vehicle, instrument, channel, method, avenue, conduit, form*, etc. A telephone is a medium (a means) for communication.

A medium can be and often is a channel for healing. There are some who don't even know they have this ability. They may be wonderful counselors who always seem to say what is needed. It is as if they are inspired to say the right thing.

Q. What is spiritual healing?

A. It is healing that is brought through from the Divine Source, or God, spirit doctors, or whichever word you wish to use, through the medium's energy or spirit healers.

Q. Is all healing received from the same source?

A. Spiritual healing indicates it comes from a nonphysical source such as as the ones mentioned. Healing is also possible through the healer's own energy field, from extraterrestrial connection, from physical intervention, and/or manipulation such as massage and chiropractics. It can also come about as a result of hypnosis, counseling, and so on. To be pedantic, we could say it is all the same source since we are all connected.

Q. What level does clairvoyance reach?

A. Clairvoyance in the main brings through information from the fourth dimension, from those still close to the earth plane, from those who have departed this life and are still in the levels of the fourth dimension. From that level, it is easier to make the connection. The medium is closer to the vibration of that level, and it is a relatively simple process to make contact and to trust the information that comes into the mind.

In general, clairvoyance work is for personal interest and not for global issues. It is often used for connection to a dear loved one that has departed or for a private issue relating to a current or past situation. We stress that this is in general, for there are always exceptions. This is usually the level aspired to during a clairvoyant demonstration. The public would be comfortable with that where they might not be comfortable with receiving a message from a higher entity or from a being not of your earth plane. We try to keep the audience comfortable and to meet their needs appropriately.

According to the level of ability of the instrument/medium to raise their own vibration that little bit higher, they can receive information or guidance from spirit guides that may be from the fourth, fifth dimension, or higher.

Not all mediums are just clairvoyant. **Clairvoyance** is clear seeing, which means a medium literally sees, either with their physical eyes or inner mind sight. Mind sight is seeing with inner sight but not with physical eyes that which is invisible to the physical world.

Clairsentience is feeling, a knowing, a sensing. One feels emotions, and/or thoughts, and has a knowing that the physical form of the spirit communicator is as perceived. In this way, the loved one can be described to a lesser or larger degree without actually being seen. The message can also be simply a knowing rather than through any other way. It may come as a telepathic link. A lot of trust in the accuracy is required for this. Often classed as a **Sensitive** is one who senses emotions, illness, or atmospheres; one who is aware without receiving actual physical sight or sound; one who receives impressions of a nonphysical presence. The medium will often use expressions such as "I sense" or "I feel."

Clairaudience is clear hearing. Those who can do this are the lucky ones since they literally hear what is to be passed on, just like a telephone communication. The majority of mediums have clairsentience—the knowing. The brilliant ones have all three abilities.

Q. Can these clairvoyants, psychics, etc., see the future?

A. First of all, the future is not set in stone. It is dependent on a person's actions and thinking and so is subject to change. They see a variety of things. What is given depends on the inquirer's needs.

They may give a description of the person you are going to meet in quite clear detail. You could say that is the future because you haven't met him or her yet. For example, the other day I was told that I would be going into a solicitor's office. I thought no way is that going to happen. I had no reason to see a solicitor at all. Then a few days later, I received a letter requesting I go to a solicitor for a matter not directly related to me. A lot of skeptics say mediums are picking up what is in your mind. That incident was not in my mind previously, so that cannot be true.

Q. What is the difference between *psychic* and *spiritual*?

A. A psychic is one who may use all or just some of the above gifts such as clairvoyance, clairsentience, and clairaudience but who is not restricted to giving messages from those who have departed this world. It may be that extra abilities are brought into play. Using those fine inner senses that we all have may be one method. In addition, a psychic may use psychometry, tarot cards, palm reading, psychic art, inspired writing, numerology, reading tea leaves, and/or dowsing. These are just some of the tools used to aid in the process.

One can be psychic without being spiritual. That is to say those psychic gifts are present but could be used for unloving purposes. I know of one lady who used her gifts to tail her husband whom she mistrusted. Another used it for selfish gain, and some use it to harm another.

Being spiritual means using your gifts for the benefit of others and having a higher objective in mind, such as service and love. One can be spiritual and yet be as psychic as a brick. If you are both spiritual and psychic, then you are a blessing to others.

Q. ARE WE ALL PSYCHIC?

A. According to *Webster*'s dictionary, the word *psychic* means appertaining to the soul in contrast to the logical, rationalizing mind. So we are all psychic if we believe we all have souls. What is generally meant by the question is, are we all able to use the inner finely tuned senses as well as the outer conscious ones? In my view, the answer is yes.

Q. CAN PSYCHIC ABILITIES BE TAUGHT?

A. Most certainly. There are psychic and spiritual development circles that can aid in this. Many spiritualist churches run open circles for you to attend and decide if you wish to learn more by joining on a more regular basis. Ask yourself, can everybody sing? Most people can sing. Some can sing well, some not so well, some are absolutely tone-deaf. Some know they can do better and wish to take lessons; others, even when they can sing and enjoy doing so, do not wish to take classes or have further training. However, every person can sing, and using that analogy, every person can be taught to use their psychic abilities if they so wish. If they apply themselves and learn, they will surprise themselves and others how well they can do. Those lucky ones who are born with their psychic senses fully functioning and are able to keep them do not need to learn since it comes naturally to them.

Q. "I am of the belief that everyone can connect with Spirit or, in fact, to any matters relating to psychic or spiritual work" (Terri). Can you ask if this is the case?

A. Everybody can if they want to. Not everybody wants to.

Q. Are abilities of the individual agreed upon before physical life starts, hence they do not need to go into a group to develop and it is spontaneous?

A. "It is not a question of whether it is agreed upon before the previous incarnation. If there is ability that has been brought down through a series of existences, whether it be during incarnation or otherwise, then this ability will remain and will be carried through with the incarnation of that individual. So the ability lies forever within, ready for awakening or for reawakening and developing. Psychic abilities are also frequently brought down through the genetic strain. In this case, it may be that the incarnating soul has chosen parents with those abilities so that it could learn and use them through its incarnation."

PSYCHIC ART

Q. Why are drawings used, and in what way? Is this what is called psychic art?

A. Someone used in this way may or may not have the ability or training to draw or paint in normal life, but when they are in an altered state of consciousness, usually through meditation or inner focus, they may do so in two ways. They have the utensils handy and either have the pen or brush moved for them by spirit with no control over what comes, or they get a mind picture and paint what they see in the mind.

When a portrait of someone's relative or friend who has died is drawn, then that may be seen as evidence that life continues and stays connected. This is especially true if along with the portrait a message is given. It is unlikely that the artist could have known what the departed one looked like.

It may be that a spirit guide is drawn. This helps the individual to connect with it during meditation. There can be no evidence that this is authentic except by personal experience later on. We all have guides, helpers, and guardian angels with us from the time before we are born. They are always around helping. (See "Spirit Guides.")

It can also be that scenes, not portraits, are drawn psychically. These drawings may carry a beneficial energy that is felt by the person for whom it was drawn. These days, many are painting beautiful colors in many shapes and forms, which give a certain vibration and feeling to those who look at these works of art. Angels too may be drawn as seen by the artist.

SPIRIT WRITING

You may get what is known as **automatic** writing where the pen is moved for you by spirit and you have no control over it. The pen does not leave the paper. This is generally in a continuous flow with no spaces or punctuation. It is not always easy to read afterward. The other way is called **inspired** writing. The thoughts come and are written as they come. You can apply the punctuation as needed. The trick is not to think about or read what is coming but let it flow. If you once stop to look and consider it, it will cease. My own messages making up the Little Owl Cards have come in this way.

OUIJA BOARDS

Q. What do you think of Ouija boards?

A. Previously called planchette, meaning "little board" in French. The board is inscribed with the alphabet and other characters with a pointer that is said to spell out mediumistic communications. It was a precursor to the Ouija board. Do not experiment with Ouija boards when trying to get communication unless you have a responsible experienced person with you, such as a medium. It only takes one who is in an open state (not grounded) to "go off" somewhere, and if you do not know how to cope with that, do not know how to bring that person back, then you are in trouble. That same person may be allowing an inferior spirit in.

You might open the door to an unwelcome guest. Not everybody who dies is good. For example, if someone is a rotten so-and-so in life, then he will likely be a rotten so-and-so in afterlife as well. If you open the door, they will love that, and you could be in for a lot of trouble. It is dangerous to use that board unless you have somebody with you who would know what to do if it all goes wrong.

READINGS

Q. What information should or should not be supplied by a medium/ psychic?

A. A great deal depends on who is receiving the information. It is easier to ask what should not ethically be given. On no account should the time of death be given. An inquirer should leave feeling more positive and better after a reading. An inquirer should be able to see a way forward after a reading. You should not give bad news since it can be made self-fulfilling. Or the news can spoil the time ahead through worry. Often a reader will be vague as to times since the future is not cast in stone. A reader can frequently see that if a certain attitude or behavior is continued detrimentally. In this case, warnings are allowable. Such as "If you continue to drive too close to the car in front, you could have an accident." Or they might psychically see a problem with household plumbing and then can say, "It might be a good idea to check your plumbing system." If they see a health problem, they could say, "When was the last time you had a health check?" Common sense is needed when judging what and what not to say.

Q. Who communicates?

A. If your purpose for having a consultation/reading is to hear from a "dear departed one," then it is likely that is the one who will communicate or have another in spirit acting on his or her behalf. If you seek guidance from a spirit guide, then it is likely this is where the communication comes from. For more information on spirit communication, see "Channeling." More frequently, the reader uses his or her psychic ability to provide the information or guidance that is sought.

Often there is disappointment when a desired loved one does not come through but a more distant relative or friend comes instead. A spirit with lots of energy and drive may have more chance to make himself known than one who is less pushy. There are reasons why some do not make it until later.

Those who give readings may operate on several levels, and much will depend on the intention and need of the sitter/inquirer. There are many variables.

Q. How can we know who to go to when we decide to have a reading?

A. Go by recommendation. That's your best bet.

Q. What if you don't know where to start?

A. Ask around. Somehow you will find the right person when you have a need. Somehow you get to know. There is a reason for everything.

Q. Is a reading helpful?

A. It can help make a situation clearer where there was confusion before. It should help you to find a way through, to make a decision regarding a course of action. It should definitely not make decisions for you or tell you what to do but help you to find your own way more easily. It can reassure you that a departed loved one is all right and happy. Some readings may be considered as spirit counseling. You should feel better after a reading than before it. You ought never to conduct your life according to a reading unless it feels right for you. You alone are responsible for your life and your decisions.

Those who give readings may operate on several levels, and much will depend on the intention and the need of the one coming for the reading.

GENUINE OR FRAUD

Q. Some believe that mediums and psychics are in the business to fool the public and to make a lot of money out of them. Are they all genuine?

A. Personally I have not met a rich medium. This is not to say that they don't exist. Charlatans exist in all fields of work and enterprise. However, most mediums I know live in modest accommodation, even the top international ones. They are not in it for the money, and with the hours put in, you wouldn't go cleaning for the money that they get. So why do they do it? Most simply they want to help others or to share in their wonderful experiences. It is a desire to do something to help people out of their difficulties. That is the prime reason they do this, to genuinely help their fellow man.

Sometimes, and I have to be honest here, they are so good at what they do that they can get to feel overly important, and an inflated ego comes in. The motive for doing what they do subtly changes. It can change from genuinely wanting to help another to showing how good they are and what they might earn. They feel great and get a following and start strutting. If this gets out of hand, the spirit link, what I call "headquarters," may take action and gradually withdraw the abilities. The medium is then left with no connection. It can happen then that mediums having been great with a wonderful gift suddenly find that it has been withdrawn. They find it hard to admit or even recognize that.

The vast majority of psychics and mediums are genuine. They have to trust what they receive from the spirit world or they couldn't work at all. They can be wrong at times. It is not easy to pick out of the ether information that needs to be interpreted accurately by the mind.

Q. What happens if a medium doesn't make any connection with the spirit world when he or she has been invited to do a demonstration and the expectations are high?

A. The worst thing they can do is to pretend they are getting something they are not and make something up. If they do this, they will be very quickly found out and lose credibility, and nobody hears about them anymore. The best thing for them to do is admit they have nothing and give a talk instead. They will be respected for that. Everybody has off days! It takes a very strong person to stand up before an audience and say, "I'm sorry, but I'm not getting anything." When that happens, you will know you have a great and honest one before you, because it won't be like that for them every time. You will get wonderful mediums of course who go on and on and who are lovely people and very humble.

Q. Why do they charge if their main purpose is to help others?

A. If they have given up their employment to do the work they are best at, they still need an income. The bills still have to be paid, and they have to eat. You would not go into a shop and expect to be given an article without paying for it. It has also been recognized that if something is given freely, it is not always appreciated. The majority of mediums, though it has to be said not all, charge what the general rate is in their area. It is worth noting that it is rare for a worker in this field to be fully occupied each hour and each day, month in and month out. To do so would exhaust most. Therefore, the income received has to be spread thinly over a lengthy period.

Many mediums who work in the spiritualist churches receive nothing more than a cup of tea and biscuits. Those who give themselves over to serving others in this way know quite well that integrity is all. They believe that what goes around comes around and the growth of their own soul is paramount. Therefore, if they knowingly deceive, they are aware they will not escape the consequences in a later life.

SITTERS

Q. What is the role of the sitter as one coming to a reader or channeler?

A. Relax and allow the medium to proceed in his or her manner and time. Have in your mind what it is you want out of the reading. Do not expect your first problem to be discussed at once. If you have several problems or issues, you may not get them all sorted in one sitting. Have patience. Do not attempt to confuse the reader, but let them know when they are correct. Be willing to verify and show that the reader is on the right path without giving information. Be fair! Expect good and try not to be skeptical. Talking a lot or interrupting throughout the reading can break the link. Try not to have an attitude that puts up a stone wall between you and then expect the medium to break through.

SPIRIT ANIMALS

Q. Do animals keep the connection with us when they die?

A. Animals are connected by love. They often make an appearance in spirit form during a reading, a clairvoyant demonstration, or during a group session. Spirit guides have said that they can manifest the form of a loved animal for a person if it is deemed to be of help. Quite frequently, groups or individuals feel an animal from the spirit world around them.

Q. Why do we sometimes get an animal instead of a guide during meditation?

A. A Native American or shaman will often present themselves as an animal before they make their own form evident. For example, a bull sitting down could represent a Native American named Sitting Bull. Seeing an owl can represent wisdom being sent to you.

Q. Do you think we create thought forms of guides as vehicles for knowledge as opposed to them actually existing? Is it maybe our higher consciousness that is manifesting as a vehicle we can accept? Are they entities that exist in their own right, or is it something we create?

A. It is a mixture, for if you consider the total consciousness, it is all merged and connected as one anyway. You will have guides who have been with you in a previous life and have been real beings and so exist. The question has been asked why guides so often present themselves as Indians, Chinese, Greek philosophers, Biblical characters, etc. The answer was very clear; they can present themselves as they wish, but if they were to do so as an ordinary man in the street, you wouldn't take much notice and it wouldn't make the same impression or have the same impact.

In our conditioning, we take more notice of those who we think had wisdom, such as the Ancient Chinese, the Ancient Greeks, and Biblical characters and so on. They are those we might wish to listen to now. Often a guide will present himself in the form where he had a life during which he achieved the most learning and wisdom. He had been many things but will choose a culture that you can resonate well with. The more dramatic they are, the more you will take note. So yes, they will manifest as a form you can accept.

ANIMAL SOULS

Q. Are animal souls different from human souls?

A. "Animal souls regroup as a group soul. They are different and yet very much alike. They hold love more strongly in their soul being than humans do, all animals, not simply your domestic cats and dogs. They have strong connections with the human race; they frequently rejoin them in the spirit world when both parties have departed. They regularly connect with their living humans even whilst in the spirit form. They are separate in form.

Q. May we interact with our pets whenever we wish? May we have the same loving relationship with them? Do we recognize each other and want to be together on the other side?

A. You cannot break a love bond even after death of either one. Thinking of them brings them close to you. Pets often visit those they love who are still alive long after the death of the pet. This applies even to horses and some other animals. Of course you will recognize each other when you are on the other side. I have seen my mother in the spirit world with her beloved ginger cat.

Q. What happens to our pets when they die? I've just had to have my beloved toy poodle Ebony put to sleep. I miss him so much. Is he looking for me in heaven? Does he realize he is dead? Is he following me around wondering why I'm ignoring him?

A. Your beloved Ebony does not feel separated from you, for from his perspective, you are still there. He is still around you even though you cannot see him; therefore, he is not confused. He does not have the mentality to wonder if he is dead or alive since he knows he exists and therefore *is*. He is perfectly happy.

Q. Do animals evolve in the same way as we do in a soul way to raise the consciousness?

A. "There are many levels of soul for the animal, according to species. All are part of the creation, and all have spirit within, no matter how lowly. But as far as consciousness and intelligence goes, you would not consider that the lowly worm has the same soul consciousness as that of a dog or a horse or a bird or a mammal of the sea. You understand the difference? So yes, they do have souls and they do have consciousness, but they have degrees and many levels according to the kind of animal. They too as soul, as spirit need to progress and will in time.

The consciousness of their existence is not readily available to them for where there is consciousness, there becomes a will and a desire to know more. That is what differentiates humankind from the animal kingdom. Humankind is aware that there is a future, is ready to ask questions, to make inquiries, to learn. An animal is content to be, to act instinctively, albeit with feelings of love and compassion also. It is limited and does not inquire from whence it comes and where it will go after its death. There is a vast difference and will always remain so.

Q. Will there come a time when they will be aware, or will things stay like that?

A. "If the Creator decides to invest creatures with a consciousness of the divine spark, then yes, it will change. The decision rests with the Greater Beings. It needs to arrive within soul consciousness of animals. Certain creatures have this, but that is very limited. It is a limited consciousness of something greater that is not clearly understood by them. You might say that some of these creatures are more highly evolved than yourselves in certain areas, but missing other areas that you have. As we have said before, there is never one answer that sweeps across the board. There are degrees, grades of understanding, and elevation.

"Elephants are highly evolved souls, as are the whales and dolphins. It is interesting to note large creatures are often those who have highly developed spiritual souls. We cannot tell you the reason for this simply that this is how it is. You have the horse as a highly developed soul and many of your domestic animals also, but along their own chosen path.

"Within their understanding and soul grouping as one big mind, their aspiration is still to develop and to proceed to a higher state. Often they need to regroup to understand this. It is very similar to a swarm of bees, how they interact with each other and act altogether, or a flock of birds, or a shoal of fish. They come together and operate as one mind and interact together. So it is a need to operate differently according to the environment and the form they have taken, and for survival. It is not a full answer we understand that, but suffice to say that all beings have souls. They are all part of the Divine Source."

Q. What is the role of the animal world on our earth and in the realm of spirit?

A. To help us learn how to appreciate our vital connection with all living things.

Q. Do our animals choose us before they come to the earth plane like our children do? Do our animals have past lives?

A. I really do not know. Sorry.

Q. If third density is ending, what will happen to all the animals on Mother Earth?

A. The different densities all exist at the same time and so do not end. Animals will continue to exist in all dimensions as part of the necessary chain of life wherever it may be and however it may be.

SPIRIT GUIDES

Q. The guides? Are they someone who has known you before?

A. Some, but not all, of the guides have been with you in past lives and know you well. They may have debts to repay you from those lives together, and this is one way they can do this and move on themselves. As you become more psychically and spiritually aware, you will get guides of a higher vibration who are able to give more philosophical or meaningful help.

You don't have just one guide. You will have a succession of guides according to where you are in your need, your spiritual progress and awareness. You will have a personal one who has been with you all the way from the beginning. He is sometimes called the Gatekeeper or your guardian angel. He will have helped you decide where you are going to be born, what kind of life you are going to have, etc. That is your personal guardian angel. You could compare him to the headmaster of teachers in a school. He will make sure that the right teachers you need will be there when you need them. Supposing for example you need a teacher to help you through a relationship, especially if you have had a succession of bad experiences. There will be a guide to help you through that.

If you have a need to resolve a problem or situation around you, then the helper will pass what aid or guidance they can give through the medium to transmit the help that is required. They will never tell you what to do. They will guide you. It is like going to a counselor who helps you find a way out of the problem.

Q. How does guidance manifest? Does it come as a thought, as intuition? How do you know you have a guide that is helping you with a specific problem?

A. It depends on your level of awareness, which is why it is helpful to attend spiritual and psychic development groups. Often it is your own link with your subconscious that helps with a problem if you have asked for it. If you are aware and have been able to meditate, you will be able to link with your guides and converse with them for yourself without the need for a medium or reader. Meditation can open up a whole new world.

If you are not meditating or psychically aware, they may make their guidance known to you through dreams, intuition, or gut feeling. They are very good at making sure you see a book you should read or person you should meet. You are helped in so many ways. You are put in places where you are meant to be. Nothing is by chance. They will act where it is important for a certain part of the jigsaw to fit, but not where it is unimportant. **Guides are for spiritual development, not material development.** They are not interested in whether you buy the right car or not. Guides are our teachers to some extent. We however have to go to the school if we wish to be taught, and that means meditation.

Q. Who do you mean when you say "they"?

A. Whether you are communicating through meditation, channeling, or through a medium/reader, "they" can mean spirit guides at any level, a departed loved one, or the angelic realm, or even beings from other planets. Often this term is used even when what is received comes from the "all that is" or the subconscious mind, your own or that of the medium/reader/channeler. The subconscious mind has access to the greater consciousness.

Q. When do you know that it is spirit speaking to you and not your own self answering your questions?

A. It is the message and information that is important and not where it comes from. If it feels right and helps, then accept it. If it does not, then reject it. Your own subconscious has access to information too.

Q. Meditations bring a lot of answers, but who is giving us these answers?

A. When you receive answers, you are tapping in to the great conscious mind, and this can mean yourself, your subconscious knowing, your guides, Ascended Masters, or those in the spirit world who wish to help. What is important is what the answers are. Accept or reject, the choice is yours.

Q. Why is it so hard to connect with spirit and hear their answers?

A. It is not as hard to connect with spirit as you might think. Often you do not realize you have made a connection. Similarly the answers given do not always come direct or in words or pictures but in the things that happen later on. This can be meeting someone you need to meet to lead you to an answer or a book or sentence coming your way that provides what you are looking for. We often expect them to speak to us during meditation, but the answers to our needs can come during our normal day. We do not always recognize this.

Q. We are what we eat, some say. What about what you listen to? Is there some special spiritual music that your spiritual guide(s) prefer to hear in general?

A. Your mind as well as your body grows according to what you feed it. If you prefer a particular kind of spiritual music, then have it. It is you that enjoys and is affected and enhanced by it. Some music may assist in raising your consciousness. The guides are looking only at your soul, irrespective of the music you might play.

Q. Are there any guiding spirits in politicians, and if so, why are they not guiding them better?

A. Every soul has a guide irrespective of who they are. A guide can do nothing if not connected with and listened to. Guides wait for the call.

ON GUIDES AND COMMUNICATORS

Q. What is a guide?

A. In meditation, it is a spirit entity that works with you during the meditation process but does not necessarily speak or show himself.

Q. How do I learn to get my own communication with my guide?

A. "For each of you who ask so earnestly to be in direct contact with their guides, do realize there are more than one concerning themselves about you. Realize that your guides are communicating with you all the time in many ways, not necessarily in conversational discourse or answering every question to which you require a solution.

"Thoughts, take notice of your thoughts. Your thoughts are influenced. You have communication. Your guides will be as you conceive them to be, it is not important how you conceive them. What is important is the feeling of love; one often feels the love from a guide. It is equally important for that being who is responsible for you to feel your love. The love must be two ways; love will draw your guide to you.

"There is what one might term a team of workers. This team is responsible for answering and aiding your needs. You might say we are specializing in certain areas. There are other teams who concern themselves with another facet of your development, and as such, we are able to interchange according to that which is required.

"There is always one guide allotted to you that monitors and ensures the correct team is on call when you need it. That one guide does not necessarily need to make frequent contact with you but will do so at certain moments. Your own guide is there but is controlling the workers. You no doubt attach names to those you feel are close to you."

Q. You often refer to different terms in talking about communication with the spirit world. Please explain.

- **Collective higher mind** is when spiritually evolved minds group together and act as one mind.

- **Creation** is the original act of God in bringing the universe or the world into existence. The result of creative power acting on matter.
- **Divine Source** is a term used to define a god force or spiritual creator without referring to a particular religion.
- **Etheric field** is a universal life force. The aura or vital energy surrounding each person or things of nature. This is said to be present in all consciousness whether physical or nonphysical.
- **Doorkeeper or guardian** is a spirit being who watches over you from birth to the grave. This may be your own soul acting as a safeguard against unwanted spirit entities. It often refers to a guardian angel or guide specially appointed to you. A doorkeeper will vet spirit beings who wish to communicate or make contact with you.

Q. Why is channeled information always spoken in English?

A. It isn't, you know (*laughter*). It is in English for English-speaking people and coming through an English channel. It would be in Finnish if it were a Finnish channeler, and so on. More seriously, it is coming through as a thought form which has no language. This is why many mediums have difficulty in getting it all out in nice clear sentences. They are interpreting thought. This could account for inaccuracy in some areas. Guides work in symbolism and thought. They are working through the mind of the person doing the channeling or reading. It will inevitably carry the flavor of the channeler.

If you have a deep trance medium capable of doing direct voice, then it can come through in a variety of appropriate languages. Guides have had many lives and frequently had different nationalities with languages we couldn't understand even now. So it is useful to use thought and symbolic pictures to get a message over.

SEEING SPIRITS CLEARLY

Q. What if some people can see spirit form as clearly as I can see you?

A. There are those who see spirit beings clearly and many would like to do so. How you handle this depends on how often and how many you see. It is usually a one-off or fleeting glimpse. Often a spirit is seen out of the corner of the eye, and when you turn to see better, it vanishes. It is important that if you are one of those people who see them all the time that you do not allow them to come at inconvenient moments. Talk to them and tell them to only come when invited. I know of one lady who has them coming through her living room in a constant stream. She doesn't mind, but I don't think many would be comfortable with an invasion of strangers walking through their house.

Sometimes the spirit of a departing loved one is seen around the time of death. Be grateful for this since it is just a need by the spirit to say good-bye, a demonstration of love.

We are not surrounded by empty space. There are spirit forms and energies surrounding us all the time, and the veil between us is very thin.

Q. What happens when we move house? Do spirit friends lose track and have to find us?

A. Your helpers can be with you if you need them, wherever you are.

Q. If helpers are with me all the time, can they see what I am up to when I would prefer to be private?

A. They don't invade your privacy in that way. It is more correct to say that they are available any time. You are seen as a light, an energy form. They also do not follow you like a shadow, for they have other things to attend to. They come when needed. However, they do know what is going on in your mind and when you are thinking of them. They know you better than you know yourself.

Q. Can departed loved ones be in different places at the same time? My gran died in Australia but was seen here in England.

A. A soul can be wherever it wants to be when it is free from the physical body. It need not be tied to a place. The consciousness of a soul can be in many different places it wishes. Time and space are no barriers to the mind of the soul, departed or otherwise.

HOW SPIRITS PRESENT THEMSELVES

(During channeling, talking with Serapis Bey.)

Q. Do you ever use an actual form in your own world or have you never any need of one?

A. "In our own world? Where we are is not a place exactly but a field of energy where we recognize each other by the light body, our field of essence. We can change form as we wish in order to interact more clearly or to take on a form for pleasure. We do this when we act in union such as at a council meeting or what you might call a conference. We operate strongly through the mind as a collective most of the time.

"For our connection with you, such as we are doing now, we show ourselves as you think of us or imagine us to be. This is why many of your artists who depict our form do so in a variety of ways depending on how they personally see us. This is why we have many faces (*laughing*).

"Shall we say that when we communicate in this way, as we do to many—we told you that thought is a reality, that it created reality in matter, in the mind, and that it can create reality in the mind of another also. So when we communicate, we present ourselves to you in a form that you can recognize. This clearly indicates from which era we come and from which spiritual aspect we derive. There are those of you who can see clearly, and you would see our form as human, for we are. You may see us as a shining light, which in all humility we say we are, to enable the blind to see. We can project ourselves upon your earth in physical form as real to your eyes as you yourselves, when the occasion demands. We are not of material form, but pure spirit.

"Do know that we can also present ourselves in humble form upon your earth, such as the humble beggar upon the street, to be seen without attention being drawn, to experience for ourselves at close range, or to test the proclaimed aspirations of any individual. I think you get our meaning. There are many who proclaim their good intentions, who determine this or that and that is as far as it goes. But we give encouragement. We can be all things."

RELIGION

Q. Many people want to know about this—especially Bible-believing Christians.

The Bible does not speak of wandering or visiting spirits. As a Christian who believes in God's word and who may witness seeing, hearing, feeling, or smelling spiritual phenomenon, how do we make sense of it all? How can I as a Christian know it is OK to witness these things, when the Bible does not speak of them?

A. It is well-known that the Bible has been altered and has had many original texts deleted at various times in the past to suit the controlling powers. Much of the Bible is missing. It is also possible to interpret the words in a way that suits any particular religious belief and still find contradictory texts within the Bible that say the opposite, according to interpretation.

It is not my brief to put forward a case for any one branch of religion, but it is easy to see that there have been prophets, seers, magical spiritual phenomena events, healers, miracles, and so on written about and described in detail throughout the Bible. Did not Jesus himself say, "You shall do all these things and more"? If you act in goodness and love, you are living according to the word of God. The Ten Commandments are not a multiple choice.

Q. Why are there so many religions and gods? And who is right?

A. Religions were started by men in different parts of the world and with different cultures. They were formed and grew so that they would be accepted in keeping with the culture and belief system in those countries. All held the same desire to encourage and maintain spiritual values and obey the commandments. All were trying to be the best they could be in their own way. With the passage of time, much has been distorted, misinterpreted, and divided.

I came across this piece which says it all.

It is DANGEROUS, spiritually dangerous, to believe that everyone is wrong and you are right. When we take up arms in opposition to people and conditions, we run the risk of missing the lesson. If we judge people by their behavior, criticize them because of their different opinion and approach, it is easy to become self-righteous. We can easily identify that what we do that is correct, in the face of others whom we deem incorrect. In the process we miss the opportunity to be patient, tolerant, or co-operative. THAT can be most dangerous and damaging to the spirit.

Q. Is the statement "There are no other gods but me" a true one or just another illusion caused by ego?

A. The meaning of this was intended to be understood that all creation is God.

We are one totality as God.

CHAPTER 2

SUBCONSCIOUS MIND
AND SOUL JOURNEYS

DREAMS

Q. What does it mean when we have detailed recurring dreams that come true?

A. There are several possible answers to this question. We are in an altered state when we sleep. The conscious mind is quiet, but the subconscious is active and the soul is able to travel out of the body. It can travel both forward and back in time. Therefore when the soul is drawn to an event that has a strong emotional impact, it is remembered when the event later comes true.

There are other reasons for recurring dreams, if it applies personally. The inner you is guiding you as well. It may be trying to point out your future program of work, what your path should be. It may be bringing forward painful experiences you have had and have pushed to the dark recesses of your memory, but which should now be faced. It is kinder and gentler to bring buried emotions through dreams before they are dealt with in conscious life.

We are all linked to the total consciousness that exists everywhere, the "all that is" that has no time. Some of us are able to tap into this consciousness while sleeping. The soul will be drawn to that part that is of interest. This may be a mission through life or a field of work we should be looking at.

We may be drawn to an event that has a strong emotional impact, as we have already said.

Q. I had a recurring dream for a whole week that later came true in fine detail. Why is this? Was I being warned, and what should I have done about that? It was to do with an accident involving my son. At the time of the dream, it was set in a village I had not been to ever. Then the event did take place much later when I had moved to that village.

A. It may have been guidance trying to draw your attention, to prepare you or warn you of the event. Guidance can come from your own soul consciousness or from your guides. Another suggestion is that you were regularly astral traveling to the event in the hope that you could change it.

Q. Does everybody have the capability to connect with the spirit world?

A. Of course. It is simply that some do not realize this or have no interest in doing so. It is not that they cannot or that they are blocked from making the connection. Others are simply happy to live their lives without this connection on a conscious level. All make connections while they are in their sleep state. It is therefore important that there be given sufficient hours of sleep for this to take place. On a soul level, much counsel is given to you. Much information is fed to you, much encouragement also. Your sleep state is as important as your waking state.

Q. Is this brought through by dreams or straight to the mind?

A. Directly to your inner consciousness, frequently through dreams. If you learn to interpret your dreams, you will learn much that you can bring to your fully conscious state. Frequently you are given information through dreams as an alternative method when you are not meditating at all. You receive greater advantage through meditation in that you are aware on a conscious level what it is you are receiving and so can put it into good use. So many forget their dreams.

LUCID DREAMING

Q. What can I do about making use of my dreams? I often know I am dreaming while in that dream state.

A. This is called lucid dreaming. During this kind of dream, being aware gives you the chance to direct events in it to your advantage or liking. You knowingly take part in how it develops and are able to take conscious control over your dream. It is an extremely vivid and wonderful dream state in which you can make your every wish come true, every single night! The easy way to do this is to tell yourself regularly, "I will remember my dreams," especially just before you go to sleep. This plants the intention in your subconscious. Also, keep a clipboard by the bedside so you can write down your dreams when you wake up. If you have woken during the night and realized you were dreaming, don't wait till morning. Write it down while still in bed. Discuss your dreams whenever you can, to reinforce the message that dreams are important and must be remembered. Your subconscious will attend to it. If you can't understand the dream, then ask the question during meditation as to what it meant.

If you want to learn more about lucid dreaming, there are many Web sites that you can go into to know this more fully and train you.

MORE ON DREAMS

Q. Are dreams of personal significance or just a dream?

A. All dreams that are remembered clearly are of significance. It is the interpretation that you put upon it that creates significance. It is a link to the subconscious. It matters not the content of the dream. What is important is what you read into it. The subconscious gives you a clue, what feels right to you. If you feel happy with your interpretation, then that is right for you. A dream is merely a utensil; it is what you do with that utensil that is relevant to you.

Q. Dreams are beautiful, living them even better—do dreams or recognition in the night disappear little by little when you hit "the right path"?

A. Parts of the dream become vague when you wake with every little movement of the body until the content of it is lost. This is why it is helpful to write notes of the dream on waking and before you get up, even in the night.

DÉJÀ VU

Q. I often feel as if I have been somewhere before when I haven't, and I've known what is to happen next. This occurs even for inconsequential things. What is this?

A. This is déjà vu. Literally it means "already seen" or knowing perfectly what will happen next. As we have said, when you sleep, the soul consciousness is able to travel out of the body and travel through time and place. It makes many journeys, some of which are not of particular interest. Just as when during sleep, we (astral) travel through time around the country—for example, we pass many villages and see people etc. Our subconscious notes what we see, and when we come upon the same thing in our conscious state, we recognize it. Time is fluid.

It is interesting to note that frequently when I am conducting a guided meditation during sessions with a group, some are already ahead of where I am going to take them. They are waiting for me to arrive and know exactly what I am going to say next before I even know it myself. This to me is evidence that the subconscious can travel ahead through time.

Those believing in reincarnation theorize that déjà vu is caused by fragments of past-life memories being jarred to the surface of the mind by familiar surroundings or people. For many of you in the physical form, it depends what you are doing at night. There are many who astrally travel, and this is a different thing. They are simply taking their astral form on a journey while maintaining close connection with the earth and visiting this or that person wherever they happen to be. They don't leave the earthly plane, and so they can be quite tired when they return because they are active in this other endeavour.

From a spirit communication:

I have someone from a future time who has been here communicating with us before.

"You were speaking of sleep and what happens in that time. We can tell you that we invite you when we need you in your nonbody state. We invite you to our future time. We are allowed this for brief episodes so that you might catch glimpses of what is ahead, to encourage your soul in your future roles. This is intended to be encouragement, not a deterrent to continuing. We are not allowed to give you lengthy episodes for this would direct your approach to your life too much. So when you travel at night, it is not simply to be of assistance or for nourishing your soul or to go to the halls of learning, as you do. It is also to give you glimpses of the future. Therefore, when you arrive in the future as a soul, much will feel familiar to you."

ASTRAL TRAVELING TO OTHER REALMS

Q. What is astral traveling, and why don't we remember our journeys?

A. Can you imagine what it would be like to be two different people at the same time? Your mind would be focused on what you had done during the night, and you wouldn't function very well during the day with this life, and so you would get a little complicated. Life in your third-dimensional form is hard enough to deal with. Many of you rush around trying to get this that and the other done, saying there is never enough time. Imagine how you would manage if your mind was also constantly on what you did at night.

What probably could be helpful to you might be the odd glimpse rather than the whole thing. Amnesia is for your protection, not because it is withheld or for any other reason. It is simply so that you can focus on your "now." You are constantly in and out of another dimension. You may not realize this for it is so fleeting. There being no such thing as time. You are indeed quite often busier at night than you are in the daytime, and you might say, "Is that at all possible?" Time has a different meaning when you are not in physical form.

Q. Do we work for others at night in our astral journeys?

A. When astral traveling / leaving body at night, many carry out healing or rescue work. Those who actually leave for another dimension to work on a much different plane of endeavour may have left the earth plane completely. They will be energized, and the physical form will be totally inert while they are gone.

Those of you who wake up flat on your back in the morning have quite frequently been very busy elsewhere, for the physical body left behind is completely still and stays that way until you return, until you wake and start moving about.

One way to see if you are out of body while you sleep is to place a crystal on your solar plexus as you go to sleep on your back. If it is still there in place when you wake, then you have been out of body. This doesn't work if you sleep curled up or on your side of course. Might be worth a try?

So there are different degrees depending on who you are, what level of advancement you have, what your soul's purpose is. There is not one short answer to this. Yes, if you are tired when you wake up, you may have been quite active; but on the earth plane—probably bossing somebody around somewhere (*laughing*)—it takes energy, you see, when you're still in the energy of the earth even while astral traveling.

CHAPTER 3

CHANNELING

A spirit entity that wishes to communicate with the physical world using your vocal chords.

Q. What is channeling?

A. Channeling can mean many forms of connecting with spirit. This is on a mental, telepathic plane. However, that apart today it is generally understood that it means allowing vocal spirit communication to come through you while in an altered trance state. It is using an individual as a conduit, using telepathy. The person can be called an instrument, a channeler, a medium, or whatever word you like to use. Channeling is allowing thoughts and information or anything spirit wishes to impart by entering the subconscious mind of the conduit, and it is then being vocalized in the language of the conduit. Not all channelers are English of course (*laughing*), and the words will be produced in whatever language is appropriate to those listening.

There are different levels of trance channeling. The deepest level is a state where the channeler is not in control of what comes through and is not aware of anything around him or her while in this state. The spirit takes over the body and voice of the medium. The medium has no memory afterward of what has taken place.

Another lighter state is more common. This is called light trance where the medium is fully conscious of what is coming through but feels as if she has stepped aside and is listening to what is being said. She is in control and is able to interrupt with her own thoughts if she considers it helpful. It is very similar to being part of a conversational group with one main speaker but, while listening to him, is able to have her own thoughts and can join in if she feels inclined. Having invited a spirit entity to talk through you, you give him center stage. (Read my book *Channelling* for more information.)

The value of this is that questions may be put to the entity (spirit) by those present, which the channeler would not normally have thought of or have the answers to.

Q. Can you give your (entity's) perspective on channeling?

A. "We are ready, willing, and able to communicate through the mind of any individual who wishes to communicate with us and who has undertaken a basic knowledge of how to allow this. From our perspective, we wait for the call, the intention, and the desire to receive. The desire must come from the instrument and those around. It is similar to putting a telephone connection at an exchange, calling us up so to speak. From our point of view, we see the energy call, the pulse of light, and we respond. We respond according to the capabilities and type of information desired. We as a collective send an entity from here that is best able to meet a particular need. For example, we have a range of specialists such as scientists, mathematicians, artists, philosophers, guides, religious figures, and so on."

Q. How does channeling work from a scientific viewpoint?

A. "If we are not speaking here of vocal channeling, then we would say that it would be more correct to say that we 'seed the mind with ideas.' This can be done in the dream state or having a eureka moment for inventors, scientists, etc., to those who have the ability to understand and absorb.

"For vocal communication as with channelers, the level of vibration is paramount. All atoms, molecules are in constant agitation and vibrate at a rate which you would call is in the third-dimensional physical level. This slow rate enables the physical form to be seen. This is the nature of science.

"When the channeler is able to raise that level so that these same molecules and atoms vibrate much faster, they are nearer to the vibrational rate of the entity they wish to connect with. The faster rate generally cannot be seen by physical eyes. We will give you the analogy of a radio that has access to many stations. The slightest twiddle of the tuning knob will send you to another station. You need to fine-tune to the station you require. It is all there, but it requires delicate fine-tuning to the channel that is sought. So if it is a scientific station you require, you set that intention, and it is the mind that selects that particular band or wavelength. Scientifically speaking, it is to do with wavelengths and direction and tuning in specifically to what it is you wish to receive. The intention and desire is important for it draws in the very information that is sought.

"We need a mind that is able to receive our thoughts telepathically and present them in a way that can be understood by those present. If a channeler receives information she has no understanding of, she cannot produce an interpretation. It would simply be ignored and washed away unless the instrument is a deep trance channeler."

Q. Why are some afraid of this kind of work?

A. "Those who have fear within them will have fear no matter what is presented to them. Not all entities who wish and are able to channel through are experienced, and they too must learn how. Some of the new guides come in a little too forcibly when entering the physical body of the instrument, causing a shock to those who are unready. It is very physical, and they feel the intrusion of another soul entering them. For those channelers who are prepared and who know that this is to be welcomed, there is no concern.

"If entry happens and is unwelcome, then all that channeler needs to do is to tell the entity to leave, and it will. On being told, it will leave immediately, having entered too fast."

Q. Will channeling become an everyday thing?

A. "It could be so, but it depends on each individual's desire. What you are really asking is, will people be in constant communication? We say no, it will not be that commonplace. You will still need to have the intention to communicate with a mind not in physical incarnated form. We will take you back to the analogy of the telephone. If you wish to be in contact with someone, you dial or you tune in to your Internet. If you don't, then there is no contact. It can become commonplace in the same way that your Internet is, but it depends on the individual wishing to connect.

"The advantage of channeling is that it can enhance your life, guide you, and give you information that you could not find anywhere else. It can encourage, inspire, uplift, and give you love. That is the purpose of channeling.

"We act as teachers, but you would not wish to have your teachers with you all the time. Having been taught, you are then expected to go out and consolidate in your life what you have learned. So yes, there are some who wish to be in communication all the time, but we do not encourage that. Your soul's progress is up to you. It is up to each individual to make its own decisions and choices. We are not allowed to take you by the hand every step of the way, for you would not grow if we did that. You would be like little children who always have mommy alongside.

"There are those who say that they have 'contact with their guides' all the time whenever they need it. What they may be in contact with is their subconscious soul mind, and they will be in touch with their inner selves to a high degree. That is all to the good and is to be applauded. Guides are there to guide and not to make decisions for you."

Q. Who can one connect with during light trance channeling?

A. A great deal depends on the level of awareness the channeler is at. In the early stages of using this ability, it is usual for a guide to communicate. Later, it can be a philosopher, a recognizable personage from a past time, a sage, an angel, an Ascended Master, or an extraterrestrial. It is generally higher than the astral plane, which is where we go initially when we die. The astral plane is where we can connect with loved ones from our lifetime.

Q. Why is it helpful or important to have someone channel?

A. I have been told by guides, or whoever is communicating, that they need to hear from someone incarnated as much as we feel the need to contact spirit. They need us because without a physically incarnated vehicle to transmit their thoughts to and through, they cannot reach those who do not meditate or connect for themselves. They wish to impart information or philosophy that will be of assistance in our lives. You could say that channelers are the go-betweens, the intermediaries.

The vibration of the channeler must be in tune with the entities they wish to communicate with. If the channeler's level has not yet reached the vibration required to make contact with high celestial beings, then they can work at this, either by themselves or within groups.

Q. What advice would you give to someone who wishes to learn how to channel?

A. When you open yourself to channel, do say a prayer before you begin. The first step is to learn how to meditate. Relax the body but keep the mind awake. The mind is going to be your intermediary. (See my book *Channelling*.) Remember it is a telepathic process, so you must use the mind. You learn how to speak aloud what is happening, and soon you will find there is a changeover and it becomes a two-way conversation. There will be a subtle interaction so that it happens before you realize.

It is a process that can be learned by anyone wishing to apply themselves seriously with dedication. Aim for the highest good of all and not just to show how clever you are. When you do it because nobody else can, and this makes you feel overly special or superior, then that is the wrong motive. You would draw to you an inferior spirit who will flatter you and tell you how fantastic you are.

If you wish to know who a true guide is and who is working for others, you will feel strong love, there is no judgment. Most of all, there is no flattery, and they will not tell you how wonderful you are. Make sure your motive for receiving information is to benefit others as well as yourself. Then you will draw to you a like-minded entity, and you will feel amazing. The energies that pass through you will elevate you. The atoms and molecules that make up your body will be in a better shape, and you might even live longer.

Q. What is so difficult about making direct communication?

A. "Communication is for those who are willing to listen and also for the listener to interpret according to his own beliefs. The same words spoken, heard, or felt or received by thought may be interpreted in many different ways according to the heart and mind of the one listening and receiving.

It is important that we present knowledge or an idea or a feeling in such a way that it is open to interpretation. It is not to be otherwise or, as you might say, dogmatic.

"We attempt to put thoughts forward as ideas to be digested, debated, and argued over and controversial. This in itself creates far more interest, far more discussion and awakening of minds than anything that is stated too rigidly. There are even times when the thoughts presented can be interpreted in a completely opposite way to the intention. This will happen when the mind of the receiver does not wish to receive what is presented and will as a result manipulate and reverse the idea to his own desire.

"There are many occasions when we use mind pictures. It is a well-known fact—is it not?—that the eye sees only what it wishes to see and is able to completely ignore what it does not recognize or wish to see. This is also true of the inner mind. This may help you understand why there are many who cannot receive what we wish to impart and many who receive in a different way (to that intended). It is not for us to impose or obligate any of you to receive that which you are not prepared to accept. We do our best."

Q. When you speak, do you speak from your own wisdom, or do you abide by an ethical code that is agreed among yourselves?

A. "We speak for all. We have all reached a certain level of understanding. There is not the discordance that exists in the minds of men. There is, however, much debate, much passing over of ideas and format, and we project, plan, and discuss and, by that, enhance our own thinking. But there is always understanding and compassion for another's viewpoint. It is essential that we understand that there are many different conceptions of one idea—it is not what you would term a discordance or disagreement. It is conception of presentation of one certain idea.

"It [communication] is according to any given situation and to meet the minds of those posing the questions. It is similar to providing food for, shall we say, an infant or a child—you would not present food of a nature that was indigestible or too difficult to absorb into the system of a child. However, if it were to be an adult, a mature person, a mature-thinking mind, then the question could be responded to in another manner and the food would be more easily assimilated without causing a blockage. Then again, there are minds of great ability to absorb and bodies which are cast-iron, you might say. We could present what is to be given in another form. We can adapt and do not mind repeating and repeating. This, after all, is the aspect of teaching, is it not?"

Q. As we gather and communicate with you, do you gather and communicate with others who are further advanced than you?

A. "We do indeed gather together, and we like your attempt to make communication for greater wisdom. A lot of the wisdom we gain must come, as for you, through our own thought patterns, through our own learning, our own studies. We, like yourselves, must make the effort, must learn together, and must gain from our experiences. There are times when those who have gone further encourage us and give us teachings and join us. It is a great joy, a great honor that they do so. We are very, very happy when this is so. But we have to put in the effort, and we do not receive the assistance we need or desire unless we have merited it. It is not there just for the asking, which might come as a surprise to you. It is not presented on a plate—it must be merited."

THE MIND AND THE BRAIN

Q. We are told that the human brain is divided into two, and yet only about 10 percent is in use. Most of the messages received have been about communication. Is this communication only to one part of the human brain, such as one side that is not used practically at all? Subconscious thoughts are in the other half, am I right in saying that?

A. "There is confusion here between mind and brain. Thought is entered into the mind and then processed by the brain. The thought does not enter the brain without passing through the mind, and so you are correct in saying that one part of brain is more receptive to thought, ideas, and shall we say, fantasy; and the other part deals more fully with the rational and the logical side of things.

"Thought would be entered into the mind, and the use that is made of these thoughts depends on how utilized your receptive brain is. Whether it is retained and acted upon will depend upon the ability of the individual to interpret and accept or reject according to development in these areas.

So you are correct in saying that those who do not develop the receptive side will receive less in understanding. However, we must differentiate between the brain and the mind, for there is an inner self that does not operate on brain. It does not operate on the physical, and all is received by that inner self. All is there waiting to be processed. Your brains are but tools."

BRAIN EXERCISES

Q. We have heard of exercises for the brain to help develop the brain to enlarge parts of the brain that had not been developed. Are we to be permitted to know of these exercises?

A. "We are preparing those of you who we feel will be receptive to growth of this nature. We are in a position of having to decide which of you will use the benefits with wisdom. It is known that there are those who have these abilities but who misuse what has been given to them, and then it works against the overall general progression. It can be similar to putting a bomb in the wrong hands, or development in the hands of those who would misuse it for ill gain.

"So we choose wisely if we can those who are able upon receiving this preparation that would be given them, who will utilize this to better the world in which they live and encourage others by the wisdom that they are able to impart. If you are given knowledge, it is your responsibility and not anyone else's to use the knowledge with wisdom. The knowledge in itself is not sufficient.

"We are merely developing physically those areas so that you will discover that you are able to receive us a little clearer. We are speaking of a knowing, a reception of thought that we are able to impart through the mind. We are aware that there exists among you in quite substantial numbers those who are gifted in receiving information and yet impart this in a way that would not be condoned by us, for they are not acting wisely."

Q. Before you go, could I ask just one more question about the brain exercises? You say that chosen people will be given these. Is this to be in the near foreseeable future, and will we know of these people?

A. "It has already begun. Changes require time and have already begun. We have in the past stated this. Changes are in progress, and they will be assisted by the children to come who will arrive complete with some of these adaptations already in place. Those who are receptive will be feeling the changes. We merely require these ones to make themselves available by means of meditation and quiet moments when the mind is not active.

"Changes are already taking place. In some at a gradual pace, and in others there is acceleration. It depends upon each individual. There are many new to this world who are complete with the change. There are many opportunities available through your Internet dealing with brain development. Make use of them."

ON WISDOM

Q. Would you clarify what wisdom is, because it seems to me that if a person's brain is enhanced, then that surely better enables a sensing and a knowing that leads to a greater appreciation? So surely wisdom built upon a grounding of knowledge would enable that person to be good and loving and wouldn't be in danger of acting foolishly.

A. "It is quite clear. Wisdom comes from another area other than your thinking processes. Wisdom comes from an ability to choose between right and wrong. It comes, if you will, from your soul's experience. The ability to decide what is correct and what is not correct. It is not so much the knowledge itself as how the knowledge is utilized.

"We will give you an example. Supposing you were given information that a person was to become ill, suffer, and die. Now you must decide in your wisdom what you must do with that knowledge. This comes from your soul's knowing, not from your mechanical brain. It comes from feelings. *Wisdom* is the only word that fits here. It is for you to decide how or whether to impart the information that you have."

POWER OF THE SUBCONSCIOUS MIND

Q. Do we use our minds enough to get what we want?

A. The mind is very powerful, and if we are persistent enough in our asking, it will provide. Be careful what you ask for. I remember the case of the lady who felt she was at the beck and call of her large family. Her constant cry was "If only I had someone to wait on me hand and foot." She later had an illness that left her paralyzed, and she had to be waited on hand and foot. Another's constant wail was "Give me a break." She broke her arm. Our subconscious does not know the difference between good and bad. It acts only on what we ask or tell it. It follows that it works in positive ways too. If our self-talk is positive, then it will act on that also.

Q. Do we have to try and live completely clean, no caffeine, no alcohol, no toxins?

A. Not if you don't want to. Only you are responsible for your body.

HOW TO CREATE—METHODS

Q. On creating our own realities and using our minds, is there any technique that you can offer?

A. "Yes, certainly. It is not a question so much of the length of time employed in any one session as a constant repetition at odd moments—odd moments such as sitting on a bus, perhaps, or any odd moment where thought is not taken up elsewhere. You would be well to project your mind to your desired end and, even for a second or two, bring the image fresh to you and then let it go. It is a question of repetition, frequency, and belief that it is having an effect.

"We would say, too, that where you have an objective, which may be the goal to arrive at, and while this may seem distant to you and unattainable to your logical brain, we would advise that you visualize and create for yourself the necessary stages that would lead to your goal. Imagine in stages something that is to your logical brain more acceptable. It reinforces communication between your subconscious, your creative self, and your conscious state. The conscious mind has a tendency to reason out, counteract, and apply the brakes. Give your conscious brain something in small steps that is more acceptable and obtainable.

"A lot depends on your objective and your state of belief. You yourself must judge the level of your belief and understanding. If your belief is total and you have had experience of achieving what you desire by similar methods, then you are already able to assimilate the larger goal. If, however, you are in the experimental stage and you wish to try it out as one would dip a toe in the water on a cold day, then take it in small stages and give yourself an image and objective that is possible or not too far away from your reality. You can increase this as you go on, as you receive confirmation that what you create can indeed become reality. Your faith and your belief will grow stronger with the practice."

MEDITATION

Active meditation is mind-focused, communicating and interacting with happenings within the meditation. This is in contrast to the usual passive, emptying-the-mind method of meditation. Meditation is the key that opens the door to developing your psychic senses.

Q. Do you have a set prayer that you can say before you meditate?

A. No. I do not have a set prayer because there is always a danger that it will become a rote prayer and lose the meaning. I speak from my heart, with feeling. My prayer has a certain formula however and can be adapted to current need. My general prayer is as follows, but remember to adapt it to your own purpose:

> Divine Spirit (or Dear Father), I come to you in love. I ask for your help with the work I have pledged to do. (Insert whatever it is you want). May there be no negative influences invading my meditation, whether it be from within me or without me. May the White Light of the Divine surround me. I invite all those guides, teachers, angels, or any who wish to come to communicate with me for the betterment of all. Amen.

Meditation - Preparation of Room

Q. Can I ask your advice please regarding preparing a room for meditation. At the moment, there's only me, but I would like to pass on know-how to my sister. I don't have any crystals etc. Any suggestions please?

A. You understand that there are no hard and fast rules, but as a general guideline, this is what I do.

- Sit and get into a quiet state of mind before starting.
- Relax each part of the body.
- Imagine a different color crystal or stone in each corner of room. It is even better if you place real stones or crystals in each corner.
- Mentally run a laser-type beam of light from one corner to the other, forming a square.
- Imagine a huge crystal above the room in the center.
- Mentally connect each corner crystal/stone to the apex crystal with a laser-type beam.
- You now have a pyramid. In your mind, glaze over the sides and base of the pyramid with a wall of light.
- Say your prayer and ask of the highest (god, father, or whoever you pray to) to fill the room with love and light, and imagine a white mist or energy to flow in down through the apex crystal into the room, filling it up.

Meditation can change your life.

Q. Do you have any tips on how to meditate?

A. I use the technique where you keep the mind fully alert. (See my book *Channelling*.) This helps those who do not manage to empty the mind that is advocated so often. The body is the only part that needs to be relaxed. The trick is to give the mind something to intrigue it on your journey down to your inner being. It won't then go off and allow your thoughts to stray to mundane matters not connected with your meditation. There is not enough space here to go into this subject more fully, so you might like to read my book.

Intend to get something. Expect to get something. Your thoughts will attract like thoughts to you.

Q. Is having music on helpful?

A. Some like music; and if you do, then have it. For me, it is like having the television on while trying to focus on something else. I end up listening to the music and not focusing on the journey. If you are meditating for relaxation, then of course music is good to have. It all depends on what kind of meditation you want.

I call my meditations working meditations. I want them to tell me what I need to know. I go in with the intention and expectation of coming back with information.

Q. What happens if you get to an early point in the meditation where you do not want to open a door to go further?

A. It has never happened to me, but I do know those who get this reluctance or feeling of unease each time. There could be a part of them that doesn't want to find out about themselves, some facet of being that they don't want to face. It is the ego consciousness that is putting up a block.

It might also be fear of coming up against the unknown. Once they can be convinced that nothing can hurt them in a meditation since they are protected by their own guardians of the soul, then they can proceed. If you can't convince them of this, then tell them to flood the space they are in with light and ask for the guides to come around them.

IMAGINATION

Q. Is what I get my imagination, and is it valid?

A. The questions you should ask yourself are the following:

    a. Is what you get helpful?
    b. Have things improved as a result of what you have received?
    c. Is what you get worthwhile?
    d. Does it make sense?

If the answers to these questions are yes, then does it matter where it comes from or if it is your imagination?

Your imagination is the best thing you can have. It is your inner being, your subconscious, your soul, or your guides who are giving you these images.

They are intended to mean something to you. Messages are frequently given in symbolic language that comes in images, imagination. It is up to you to interpret what the imagination is telling you. Imagination is bringing to consciousness an inner desire and, by so doing, is making it a reality, a possibility.

Q. What importance does meditation have?

A. "It simply enables you to be unaware of your body, just as when you watch television or read a book. If you are engrossed, you are unaware of your body. Meditation is similar to being so totally absorbed in what you are reading or watching or imagining, so immersed that you enter into it and become one with what you are absorbing, whatever it is. It is very much like becoming a child again, entering fully into your imaginative games.

"Imagination is all-important and allows you to become a child again, that blissful existence where imagination is real and very much present. In that way, you can tap into your real selves and to your helpers by becoming young again, but with the experience of an adult. It can provide you with information, give you wonderful journeys, uplift you, and steer you in a purposeful direction.

"How many times do you say, 'Oh, if only I knew then what I know now, I would have done things differently'? This is an opportunity to go back into the 'then' with the knowledge of the now and understand or change the 'then' with your thinking and gain from the past so that you may bring it into the now. It is a wonderful tool.

"Do not worry if you cannot relax your body. Providing you enter fully and become engrossed in your imagination and where you take yourself, then your body will automatically relax. It will happen, providing you have total absorption. That really is the secret of meditation."

Q. How long should I meditate?

A. The length of time is not the relevant factor here. It is how that time is utilized. One can sit for eight hours or more in what may be considered to be meditation, but that very word implies a variety of states to different people. For some, meditation is merely reflecting on the nature of things and just sitting in quiet contemplation. For others, the word *meditation* implies communication with a two-way exchange. For yet others, that same one word implies taking the mind on chosen journeys.

So you see, the individual who sits for eight hours may be involving himself in more than one pattern or just one, some of which you would not consider to be a meditative state. If he feels the benefit of sitting for that length of time, then it is of course helpful and an exercise he has chosen.

For those whose time is limited, who feel they cannot allocate to themselves a fixed lengthy period for meditation, even five minutes is better than none whatsoever. In fact, it will be found that if a few minutes is given, then the desire for lengthier periods will overtake them and they will find themselves meditating for longer periods or snatching the odd few minutes throughout their day.

As I have said, there are many degrees of meditation or reflection inward. It is not essential that one particular practice alone is adhered to. The effect, the benefit, and the well-being resulting from such contact with oneself are the important factors. As with all things, the more one practices any activity, the easier and more natural it becomes, and one finds it becomes as simple as breathing and as natural.

GROUNDING AND SAFETY IN MEDITATION

Q. I have a question about how many people are slightly out of touch with the earth. We say they are not grounded, and I wondered what observations you had to make on that. Some teachers talk about the need to root deeply down in to the earth. Comment please about the safety aspects in meditation if one isn't grounded.

A. "It is a valid point and a very good question. Keeping your feet on the ground refers to living your life not only to spiritual aspirations but also to conducting yourselves according to social requirements. You must interact and relate with others around you so as not to create discord. If it were possible to grow totally in a spiritual realm, then there would have been no need for incarnation. The reason for being in your present physical form is so that you may live a physical life and attention should be given to this life. It must not be pushed to one side totally in favor of spiritual aspirations. The two should work together in equal balance.

"You ask about the safety aspect. Indeed! On entering meditation or any altered state of consciousness, it is advisable first to make application to the Divine Source or whatever name you give that source, for there is one only. Ask for negative influences to be kept away from you while you are in your altered state or at any time when you feel the need. We do not state 'evil forces,' we prefer the terms 'misguided,' 'negative,' or 'misdirected.' When a safeguard is required against these lower spirits, then we will provide it on application. You must ask for what you require and it will be given.

"It is well to be aware that in your meditations you need to be in control. Any time that you feel uncomfortable, ill at ease, or sense the presence of anything that creates a fear, then quickly ask for further protection, safeguarding. Ask in your mind for protection, and the difficulty will evaporate.

"So often we are faced with those who meditate, who are bringing up their own fears. The fears that surface often take on the semblance of a horrific being. When this occurs, do know that the horrific feeling comes from within and may be evaporated upon recognition. It is not to be feared, for you would not injure *yourself*. It is well if at these moments, after having asked for assistance, to acknowledge in your mind that this manifested object may be vanquished by recognition.

"Keeping one's feet on the ground (*smiling*). We have many helpers who are sent to you. Some wait for your return and have means of ensuring that you return from your meditation no matter how deep you go. They stand there, waiting and watching. You might not visualize them as beings, it may be an itch in the ear or some physical sensation that brings you back to your reality. We have our ways of ensuring that you return.

"It is necessary, we may add again, to ask if you have a fear of not returning, to ask at the outset to be brought safely back to your physical being in your physical environment from which you started. All that is asked for may be given."

SYNCHRONICITY

Q. What is synchronicity?

A. *Synchronicity* is "meaningful coincidence." It is when things line up for you in a way that brings meaning to life events. It is a term coined by Carl Jung that says that "meaningful coincidence **Synchronicity** is the experience of two or more events which are causally unrelated occurring together in a meaningful manner." In order to count as synchronicity, the events should be unlikely to occur together by chance. Neither of the events can cause the other.

Q. Should we take notice of chance events, synchronistic happenings?

A. Yes indeed. Synchronistic meetings are like mirrors that reflect something of ourselves. If we want to grow spiritually, all we have to do is take a good look. Some say it is the soul or our guides that are putting things in place to assist you in your journey. It is our job to notice and act on these events that seem to occur by chance. It may be the answers to questions that you have put during your mediation. I view it as being of enormous help if we recognize it as such. I like to think someone somewhere is doing their bit to help. Others say that if you need help or direction, all you have to do is ask and the synchronistic events will occur to make sure you notice that help is being provided. See examples below.

- You walk into a bookstore not knowing what to buy, and the book you need falls from a shelf and practically hits you over the head.
- You have been feeling ill with no clear diagnosis. You meet someone who knows a doctor or healer with the answers that will help you.
- You wish to join a group and you meet the one person who can put you in touch with or who invites you to the group you want.

A well-known example of synchronicity involves the true story of French writer Émile Deschamps. In 1805, he was treated to some plum pudding by M. de Fontgibu. Ten years later, he encountered plum pudding on the menu of a Paris restaurant and wanted to order some, but the waiter told him the last dish had already been served to another customer, who turns out to be M. de Fontgibu. In 1832, Émile Deschamps visited a restaurant with a friend and is once again offered plum pudding. He recalled the earlier incident and told his friend that only M. de Fontgibu is missing to make the setting complete. At that moment, a senile M. de Fontgibu enters the room by mistake.

ENCOURAGING SYNCHRONICITY

Until one is committed, there is hesitancy, the chance to draw back always, ineffective concerning all acts of initiative (and creation). There is one elementary truth, the ignorance of which kills countless ideas and splendid plans, that the moment one definitely commits oneself; then providence moves too. All sorts of things occur to help one that would not otherwise have occurred. A whole stream of events issues from the decision, raising in one's favor all manner of unforeseen incidents and meetings and material assistance that you could not have dreamed would have come your way.

PATIENCE

Q. Why are we constantly asked to be patient? It seems that we are always waiting for something to happen, and it doesn't feel as if we are getting anywhere.

A. "Do not confuse patience with stagnation. It is very easy to confuse the two. Patience if left too long at peace can stagnate, as a pool will stagnate if it does not flow. If you feel the flow has ceased, then there will be stagnation. If there is still a flow, a movement, however slight, and then you will know you are in the realm of patience. Look and notice whether there is a flow or movement or nothing. Stagnation can spread to all areas.

GUILT

Q. I've never been able to get a satisfactory answer on guilt.

A. "Guilt is conscience, it is a guide between one course of action and another. Conscience is a necessary part of development, the knowledge that one way is better perhaps than another. *Guilt* is only another word for taking a wrong choice knowingly and deliberately. Guilt is the result.

"Sometimes a feeling of guilt is misguided and not deserved. When one has taken a course that was not right for them but did not know it at the time and did not recognize that fact until later, then there is no justification for feeling guilty, especially if the wrong direction is then turned around and actions are reversed into a more favorable path.

"When you do the best you can, with the best of intentions, and yet things go wrong, you should not feel any guilt. It is only lack of experience and knowledge that has caused things to go wrong.

"Another point worth making is that when you do something with guilt or shame, deserved or not, your immune systems decrease, even with something as minor as eating chocolate."

LOVE FEELING

Q. How can the world feel love, and how can we feel it when we want to?

A. "There must be understanding between peoples. If there is no understanding, there cannot be compassion; and if there is no compassion, there cannot be love. Love is what you are aiming for.

"These words are simple, but putting it into action is not so easy. We can all speak words that are descriptive of thoughts and feelings. It is what is in the heart and deeds that carries the effect. For feeling you must have, which will show in your face, in your stance, in your being. Words are useless without feeling, thought, and intention."

Q. Some people find it difficult to feel "love and light" for others, how can we develop that feeling for everyone around us if it does not come naturally?

A. Remember if you can that each individual is having their own journey through life and, as a soul, is dealing with challenges, personality traits, and making mistakes as they go along. Think of them as souls on their way through life. You do not have to be compatible with them or like them, but you can try to feel compassion for the way they are and be accepting, not judging. Strip away the outer covering and see them as souls working their way through.

Put yourself in their position and look through their eyes. Through their eyes, look at yourself. It is not easy and takes practice.

RELATIONSHIPS

BONDING WITH ONE CHILD AND NOT ANOTHER

Q. Why would it be that a mother might feel a subconscious link or bonding on an etheric level with one child a lot more than another?

A. "There are many reasons for this. There have been in all cases unity with that child's soul in times past and will be in times future. The future is not often considered. The linking and bonding with a particular child that is stronger than that of another so that the child that is more favored indicates that there have been many more experiences in which the closeness and bonding have been of vital importance. This results in a strong emotional attachment. You could say a tie of love.

"Where another child is not receiving this close attention or feeling, there will still have been links, but it was not of a nature where it has been remembered with pleasure. It may be that the child in a previous time was responsible for bringing pain, discomfort, or displeasure or something of a negative nature to the mother. They are brought together yet again so that either the child or the mother learns to relate on a more favorable level 'to get on together.'

"What has been placed before each of them is a situation where they cannot easily move away. For example, if you were placed in a room with an individual with whom you did not feel comfortable or you did not particularly take to, you are quite at liberty to move out of that room and away from the energies of that one. Where you bear a child where you have the same distancing feeling, you are not at liberty to move away. You have been given and have taken upon yourself a responsibility to nurture and to do what society expects of you. You cannot easily escape what has been placed before you, and so you must learn to accept, to cope with, and to bring to each of you an understanding of the nature of the other.

"It is part of your learning not to be taken as a burden that has been placed upon you or something that you wish you had not had, as happens so often with offspring. This produces a guilt feeling within the parent and indeed within the child where they cannot agree to be together in harmony. It produces guilt because they feel and society demands that they should not feel this way toward a member of the family. But it happens frequently and could be viewed as a learning process, as a challenge, something to surmount, something to come to terms with, whatever way you like to interpret. View it with pleasure if you can and see it as growth."

WHY ARE WE HERE?

Q. What is the point of this life?

A. We are here to have experiences and to grow through them. Through our individual growth, we make a difference to the growth of all humanity and to the whole of creation. It is believed that each and every one of us on this planet needs to be aware that this one life is not the only one we have. This planet is given to us as a responsibility. Our lives here should be an enjoyment, but it can only be enjoyment if we have the right attitude to it. I'll give you a comparison. Imagine you are in a job that you hate going to every day. Try changing your attitude to it and you will be surprised what a difference it makes. The same goes for life. You can actually enjoy even the trials and challenges that come up.

Try for example to be kind to everyone you meet, whether they are kind to you or not. You will be amazed at the difference in their approach to you. Try scowling at somebody in the street and see what you get back. Try smiling at someone and see what you get back. It works on that level, and it works on every level no matter how difficult the situation.

Some people are here to be of service to mankind. They are here on a mission or to accomplish something to benefit others. They will generally reach a much higher level for they will draw to them superior entities who will impart knowledge to all and not just for self-interest. There are those who are self-serving or serving others.

Q. I wonder what the point of humanity is as I can see eventually we will destroy our Earth, so what was the reason for our existence?

A. First of all, we will not destroy our wonderful planet Earth. This will not be allowed, and the Earth will survive in spite of us. Remember that our existence is as souls and does not have to be on any particular planet. As souls, we cannot be destroyed. The point of being a human is to experience as much as possible and to grow through those experiences. The point of growing is to ascend to higher states of glorious being ad infinitum until we rejoin with Creation. Stay with it as it is an amazing ride.

Q. Other than the giving and receiving of unconditional love, what is the purpose of life? In other words, is *love* the only reason?

A. When you really feel love for all things, that alone is worth the ride. The purpose is to add greatness to the soul so that you might reach what you might call paradise or heaven.

Q. What is the advantage of taking material form?

A. It is only in physical form that you can experience as much and have such an effect on all around you as to make a difference to your world. While in spirit form, you cannot always connect with those still incarnated and change what you would wish to.

Q. How does someone find out / know what their purpose in life is?

A. Look into your feelings and see what makes your heart alight in joy. If you have a gift that can help others or yourself, make the most of it. Everybody's purpose for living is to learn as much as you can during your time on earth. If your interest is sparked in any one direction, then follow that interest. Not everybody has a mission and is incarnated simply to experience and to get on with others or to correct a fault in oneself. If you feel you have a mission, then have a channeled soul reading to discover what it is. (See www.little-owl.org.)

Q. What can I do when the going gets tough?

A. "We are aware that those of you on the earth plane have all had your trials and tribulations and that the going gets tough for you. The first thing is to remind yourself that this lifetime that you are incarnated into is but one and does not last forever. The only thing that lasts forever is your soul. So turn to your soul. We suggest you detach yourself when you can from the circumstances that are difficult and look inward to the calm that is your soul. While the conscious self is turbulent, worried, and preoccupied, your soul may be the calmest point of you. So it pays, does it not, to go inward on these occasions? It doesn't mean that you can change your situation, but it does mean that you can change how you view it and how you deal with it. It can provide you with serenity and peace. Others will look at you and wonder how you can be so calm when things are going so wrong. They do not know the secret of going deep within.

"So your next question might be "How can I go deep within when I have a nagging pain or getting interrupted whenever I try to meditate?" Have you all experienced that? Of course you have. In having these experiences, it is giving you understanding too, and when you have had a few gifts of a challenge and when you depart this world, you are ready, primed—you too can be guides and teachers.

"So how do you hold on when the going gets tough? You remind yourself and the soul within that you have died many times before and yet you still come back for more. So you see, these difficult times are exactly what your soul craves for. You might find that a little strange, but when you reflect on it, how can you learn to be brave when you have never had difficulties to overcome? How can you be wise if you never had problems to solve? How can you be compassionate if you have never experienced what others are going through? We do not like to think of these things as lessons; we like to think of them as gifts that will help your soul to grow and develop and become mighty as a result. Nothing lasts forever except your soul.

"Remind yourself of the times in your past when things have gone wrong. You have survived them, have you not? For here you are still; it hasn't beaten you down. This is where your free will comes in, to choose to rise above the challenges or drown in them."

CHAPTER 4

FIELDS OF INTEREST

Q. Where are our skills acquired? On earth or elsewhere?

A. Each aspect of a soul at its origin begins with a particular interest and so seeks to have learning and experience in that field. Over its lifetimes, it chooses to stay in environments and families where it can learn bit by bit and develop the skill more and more. So it learns through incarnation with that objective in mind. It may choose parentage where the genetic influence will help. It will choose to be born under a particular astrological sign to enhance its characteristic. It is a combination of things. We are speaking of one aspect of the soul, not the oversoul.

CRYSTALS

Q. Can you give us in simple terms the use of crystals please?

A. Crystals are great concentrators, storehouses, batteries, and generators of thoughts and energies. As such, they are controlled largely by the user and are receptors of energy that the user would attract by intention and thought. It is a concentration of energy in order that the thought or purpose attached to the crystal is magnified, enhanced. That is the use of crystals.

They are tools, but like every living and inanimate object, they have a force, an energy of their own in their own way. Every atom is energy and, as such, is living."

AWAKENING

Q. How long will it be before we awaken?

A. "How long is a piece of string? There will be those who will not awaken in your lifetime. There are others who are doing it all the time. It is down to each individual, but what you are really asking by your question is about mass awakening. Is it going to sweep across the land, you ask. There are more and more people becoming comfortable with the idea of a spirit world and communication with spirit. The more this happens, the more it is encouraged, and it will become commonplace. Those who are not awakened will be in the minority. It is recommended that all get on the bandwagon, wake up, and be part of all society and not on the outside. Do not worry about awakening, for it will happen.

SUDDEN AWAKENING

Q. How is it that some have a sudden awakening, and what causes that? For example, I had gone down low in my life to such an extent that I wished to end it all.

A. Some find themselves in danger, dire circumstances, despair, or alarm of some kind such as an illness or extreme accident and have what is known as a wake-up call. A physical experience can often shift the etheric body out of the physical body, and in that instant, it touches upon another dimension. It enters a world not of the third dimension. The shift or jolting is often sufficient to cause a change or a call for help. It can be sufficiently traumatic to bring an end to suicidal tendencies or despair. This is when man has nowhere else to go, and that is when he gets down on his knees and prays.

Often an experience like that triggers a need to know more, wanting to have help alongside him, to desire to assist others. It may be seen that this extreme method has been used to kick-start an individual into the role it had planned for itself before birth and then had forgotten about. It may be a method of tapping into, beginning or completing a mission that it was here for all along.

Sometimes when an individual has suffered, whatever the cause, there is compassion for others that is real and heartfelt because they have endured it themselves. This results in a wish to alleviate the suffering of those who are having similar experiences. Often this gives rise to raising awareness in others or funding for research. It becomes a reason for living, and that is what causes the soul to grow. Life is for experience of all kinds so that you might grow.

Another reason for sudden awakening may be when the Kundalini opens or when an individual has had contact with a "space brother."

GHOSTS

Q. What about ghosts or spirits who are felt to be around?

A. If you have a relative or friend who has recently departed this world, they may be felt to be around. This can be for some considerable time if the need is there by those still in body. However, ghosts are generally thought to be more ancient than that. They return to the scene of their demise particularly if it had been traumatic. What most people see is the etheric energy vision of the person that had such a strong and lasting effect on the place that it remains to be seen by those who are sensitive enough to do so. Some are capable of seeing whole battle scenes complete with horses. This vision or visions cannot harm you in any way.

SOUL RESCUE WORK

Q. What about lost souls?

A. If you are a person who is an open psychic door and is making spirit connections, you might allow somebody in who hasn't yet made it over to the "other side." The departed spirit doesn't know what to do and sometimes doesn't even know they are dead. They may be distressed or are hanging around because they are worried about the family they have left behind. When they come in to somebody, they usually come with that distress or physical ailment very evident. That can be quite frightening, especially if it is a stroke or car accident that killed them. If you are in a development circle, the medium will recognize what is happening and talk to the confused and distressed spirit and guide it over to the other side where other spirits will take over and help. If this unexpected visit happens while working with an Ouija board or in a group without experience, then it causes a lot of distress and trauma to the person who had the spirit enter them. An experienced medium or psychic is essential to deal with this kind of opening.

Q. What happens to those people who do not appear to have completely gone over to the other side?

A. Sudden or traumatic death can lead to some souls being stuck close to the earth and not going all the way to the next stage. Psychic spiritual groups or individuals are trained to connect with these souls and guide or counsel them to go to the light where they will be looked after. At times, it is a spirit being from the fourth dimension that goes to them and helps them to pass over completely.

Q. When someone dies suddenly, is there someone they know on the other side waiting for them?

A. There is always someone waiting to greet and help. Whether it is to be someone they know is dependent on the circumstances, the belief—or otherwise—of life continuing. Some people do not believe that there is anything after death. Some are taken to meet people they know after a time needed to adjust to their new surroundings.

Q. I have often heard it said that when we leave this life, someone from our human family who has already passed over comes to meet us. Is this true? Or will it be an angel/guardian?

A. It can be either, but is usually a family member.

Q. When we continue our journey in the afterlife, would we have memory of this present moment?

A. Certainly, until such time as it can be let go and you wish to move forward.

TIME OF SOUL ENTRY AND DEPARTURE

Q. When does the soul enter the body?

A. A soul can enter at conception, at any time during the pregnancy or at birth. It can also come and go during the gestation, getting used to being physical. It can change its mind and decide that after all, it does not want to stay. This is when a pregnancy can abort, miscarry, or even be a stillbirth.

Q. Wouldn't the soul know this beforehand?

A. Nothing is set in stone, and perhaps there had been some physical malfunction to the fetus along the way.

Q. Another similar question on soul entry. What stage does the soul enter the fetus?

A. There is variation on this also. There are times when the soul who has decided to reincarnate again is a little indecisive. Even souls can be indecisive and hesitate before making up the mind. There are times when this decision to incarnate or not is at the last moment and, at such times, can even be as late as just prior to the birth. This is an exception, and it is more normal that the soul makes its decision well in advance and enters the fetus at an early stage, but there is no set time.

Q. I've read that when a soul enters a body, it's a merging of soul energy and "human" energy (mind/ego). This would mean that "we" are two in one. So how much of "we" is who we are in our current life, and when we die, the soul moves on, but what happens to the "human" energy?

A. An incarnated soul is a composite of three that makes an individual who he or she is in any life journey.

1. First there is the quality of the personality of the soul gained over many life experiences. That is, a soul can on entry be a happy one or a miserable one. We have all seen identical twins even at birth, one of whom may be a joyful child and yet the other quite different. So clearly this has nothing to do with genetics or environment.

2. Secondly the genetics of the parents and past family play a strong part. This can apply to character and disposition as much as physical appearance.

3. Then as the incarnation progresses, the environment and challenges presented have an effect on the human and soul energy, making the totality of the being.

On death, the soul energy is all it has gained or lost during that incarnation. For a while, it maintains its human energy and form until it realizes it no longer needs to. It retains the characteristics, views held, and personality it had while alive until it moves on.

The genetics of the human body that it had may continue through the genetic line. If this has been improved upon during the journey, then it will have enhanced the human form in years ahead.

ABORTIONS

Q. Are abortions right or wrong in the eyes of spirit?

A. There are no rights or wrongs. It is all a matter of judgment and choices made. You are not killing a new soul. The soul that was connected with the fetus would have known when the abortion was to take place and would have left beforehand. Therefore, no killing of the soul takes place, simply an end to a part of the physical body. The soul that wished to incarnate would simply seek another mother, or even the same one at a later time.

There are always more souls wishing to incarnate than there are opportunities suitable to their requirements.

PREGNANCY TERMINATION

Q. How is the termination of a pregnancy viewed in your dimension? Is it considered wrong?

A. There is never any judgment. If the termination is in the early stages, then it affects emotionally the soul of the parent. Much is dependent on the reasons for the termination, whether it be for the sake of the unborn or for the carrier, the mother. If it is to safeguard the physical condition of the mother or the child, then it is viewed with tolerance and understanding, especially so since the child in all probability had decided to incarnate briefly for the experience only, to make contact with its parents. That contact would remain forever a bond.

There are, however, instances where the child/soul had developed spiritually enough and had decided to incarnate and live a life of difficulty through physical or mental abnormality. If there is termination, then that child/soul has been blocked to some degree. It is not too serious however, for that soul will wait for another opportunity to incarnate. It simply means a delay as the soul must wait for the correct time as well as for suitable parents. Generally, the soul chooses well and is aware prior to its decision whether the pregnancy will continue or not. However, all souls have free will, and this includes that of the parents.

Q. How do you view a woman who has had a test that says she is going to have a baby with abnormalities and she decides to terminate?

A. That is the decision of the parents. It is their free will to choose, and as such, it should be honored. They alone must come to terms with their action; it is not for any other to judge. We are not in a position to judge each other, and we each act according to our soul's pattern and intention. We consider it to be a choice that is rightfully free.

Q. Is what we call cot death caused by the soul having had the experience it needs and returning home again?

A. All souls decide when they wish to leave, and cot deaths are simply another means of exercising this right. It might just have well been another means such as pneumonia or some such other illness. The cot death is relatively quick and painless. There are times also when there has been a joint decision between the souls of those parents and the child to experience the loss of a child. There is no one set reason for events that happen. There are many complications and complicated patterns to work out, and the souls decide which most appeals to them as serving their purpose. One cannot be dogmatic and precise about dates and events and the wherewithal of such actions.

CHAPTER 5

DEATH

Q. Why it is such a struggle for some to die, as it is to be born?

A. Some hold on to life because they don't want to go. Others are fearful of the unknown. Yet others do not want to leave what they have amassed during their lifetimes. Some are reluctant to leave their family members.

Then it may be relatives who are holding them back. There was one old lady who complained that her relatives would keep on praying for her to get well. "It's so unfair," she said. "If only they would let me go."

They may not believe that it is better on the other side. Some do not believe that there is anything at all after death. Death should hold no fear. If you have achieved a state of serenity, life and death will hold no fear.

Most people don't fear death in itself so much as the way they will die. If you have managed to understand what you really are and that you will continue to exist, then even the experience of dying will hold no fear. Even if the lead up to death is a painful one, it will be easier since there is no pain in the dying. The soul is totally wrapped up in the beautiful experience it is having. It is often recognized by those around the dying person that the body itself is empty of consciousness and that the mind has gone elsewhere. The mind has gone and is oblivious of pain.

Q. What do people think about in their last hours?

A. I imagine many things, depending on their circumstances and whether they are in pain or not. Are they contented or bitter, happy or sad? They will not be concerned whether the house is clean or not. They will not dwell on whether they were burgled in the past or whether they made a lot of money or lost a lot. What is important to them is how they feel about themselves and how they have conducted their lives. The best way to feel is satisfied with a life well conducted.

It has been reported that when a person is in the last days on earth, a departed loved one is present waiting patiently to assist in their journey.

Q. Are you conscious of what is happening when you die? Are you aware of where you are afterward?

A. There are many possible answers to that question. For most, just after you die, you will be exactly the same without the pain or physical encumbrances and restrictions you had in the flesh. Many travel through what has been called the tunnel by those who have reported after a near-death experience.

The majority of people will be met and will be aware and know exactly what has happened. They will still retain the form they had while alive but, not being physical, will not have the burdens or pains of the flesh. Many feel they are still exactly the same, and this may last for a few days or longer. It is often thought that we attend our own funerals. Those who see spirit clearly have said that they have seen the departed standing at the funeral. One person told me that she saw the departed one with a clipboard, laughing and noting who was present and who was not.

Those who have had a long and perhaps painful illness are usually adapting to spirit life while still in the flesh. Since they are often on pain medication and sleeping, they do what we all do often when asleep. They travel out of the body. This is called astral traveling. This is because when the soul knows it will soon leave the body behind, it prepares for the next phase of being. It visits the other side and sees relatives and friends who are already there. It is only a question of time, and when it does come, they are on familiar ground at last, surrounded by welcoming arms.

EUTHANASIA

Q. What is the view on *euthanasia*?

A. "It is an interesting subject. We do not condemn when the person requesting euthanasia does so in the knowledge that one must die as a result of an illness and that death is inevitable. It is not counted against such as one. It may be seen as an acceptable means, a desire to escape unnecessary pain. If that soul had originally intended to experience the pain and not escape it, it could be that the pain may be endured in another existence. There are many degrees of response to this question.

"If terminating when a soul has already departed, with the physical body still functioning by means of artificial equipment, then it is totally unnecessary to prolong that life. A disconnection is not only acceptable but also advisable to facilitate the complete departure of the soul, for while it is connected by artificial means, it cannot completely leave its body. It does so only in the manner that you all experience at times in your sleep state and, for some of you, at will. There is no hard and fast rule, for each individual case must be viewed separately."

Q. Doctors who actually administer a drug to cause euthanasia. Are they classed as murderers when they go to the spirit world? How are they treated? What is the position?

A. "The position from our point of view depends entirely on the motives of each individual doctor. The motives are important. As we have said, each individual case must be looked at. Where a doctor terminates a life by means of excessive application of drugs in a genuine attempt to ease pain, out of compassion for a suffering soul and frequently at the request of the patient, this is not condemned in any way."

Q. Does anyone go to spirit before their time? For everyone who goes back, is that the right time for them?

A. "There are occasions when it is felt, not by the soul incarnated but by those who are given the responsibility of guiding and working for the benefit of that soul, that in a few cases, it can be considered that continuation of earthly existence can be detrimental not only to the soul but also to have a detrimental effect on those around. It is not always given to the soul to decide.

"We will give examples. There are those existing who create such disharmony, such malevolence, such destruction on your earth that the ill they do others is out of proportion to the ill they do themselves. It must be weighed in the balance whether that particular soul should be brought back and restarted.

"For the main body, if you will excuse the expression, if the soul decides that enough is enough or 'I have fulfilled my project or purpose in life ahead of time, so I can peaceably depart,' and does so.

"In some cases where hardship is unbearable, they can convince their innermost being that enough is enough so that their physical bodies respond to the subconscious messages and, in this way, terminate the incarnation. It is not always our wish that they do so, but free choice must prevail in the majority of cases."

Q. Is there a distinction between euthanasia and suicide?

A. "The distinction is that of human thinking. From a soul's point of view, euthanasia is acceptable by the spirit world. There are many ways to end one's life. Where it become intolerable, you may request a "walk-in" if you wish, or you may simply have the will to die and then do so. If you request the assistance of another to help you in this, it is perfectly acceptable."

Q. What do you say about euthanasia and the person that may administer it? Are they culpable in helping somebody?

A. No, they are viewed with compassion and grateful thanks if their motive is to help. "This is a very deep question, and we have to be a little careful here in what we put into your minds; you understand our difficulty, we are not allowed to direct you so that you change your thought pattern. It is up to you to decide for yourself. On the subject of euthanasia in our belief system, and we also have many, when an individual soul has reached the end of its journey in a natural way, then it should be allowed to progress to the nonphysical state, particularly where the end is inevitable.

"We do not encourage continuation for souls who have suffered so greatly that they are traumatized when they arrive in the fourth dimension. For much recovery time is needed on that side of the veil. It is much more natural that the body be allowed to die when its end has come. You understand that we are referring now to artificial means of keeping the body going longer than it would otherwise do. So in this sense, we would prefer that the end came naturally according to nature and not according to the machines that prolong life and often prolong the pain along with it. You would not do that to an animal, would you? Why do you value human souls less?

Q. Does the prolonged use of life-support machines in hospitals in any way hold or affect the spirit of the person treated?

A. "So much depends on the mind of the near-dead. It may be that he realizes he has left his old form but it is still being manipulated. His spirit will be either aghast or indifferent. It will not alter his journey but will be taken as a moment of experience. In the concept of time, what matters if you left this week or next?

"There are many souls on the other side who wish they could have gone earlier but, through the interference of those who say they wish to help, have prolonged their stay. While indeed we feel for them and for the beloved on the other side who are waiting for their ailing relative—for they wring their hands and say, 'When is he (or she) going to be allowed to come to us?' They wait a long time, and they suffer too in what they see."

THE FOURTH DIMENSION AFTER DEATH

Q. Do we all go to the same place in the fourth dimension after death?

A. There are many names for the places we go to after death. The fourth dimension is just one of those names. There are many spiritually advanced souls who are simply passing through the spheres on their way to a higher dimension. Some scientists may decide to join other groups of scientists in a higher place to continue the work there.

There are various levels in the fourth dimension. Most go to the level closest to the earth-vibration level after death so that you can be gently adjusted to a nonphysical state and rejoin loved ones who have previously departed. How long you stay there before moving on depends on many things too various to go into in this book.

Q. When we reach the fourth dimension, would we not be speaking but be speaking telepathically, is that right?

A. You will still speak if you so desire, there will be language in speech. However, there will also be transference of thoughts, recognition of what is going on in another's mind. This will not be invasion, for where action is correct, there is no fear of interaction with another's mind. There need be no fear. Emotions also will be felt and will be evident.

SUICIDES

Q. What do you say about people who commit suicide?

A. There are many reasons for committing suicide. It is the state of spiritual growth that counts here. How close is the soul to the goodness that they are trying to achieve? Not all people who commit suicide can be conceived of as bad, and they are not. They are just suffering as incarnated souls and need help. They are not judged adversely here because they have committed suicide. They will get much help and support. It is known that they will have to come back at sometime and face whatever it was they couldn't face in that incarnation. There is great feeling of compassion for them. There is no judgment either when the cause of the early death is misuse of drugs. Drugs steal the mind.

Spirit told of one case where an evolved soul as a young man committed suicide to have the experience and understand it so that he could help other suicides when they arrived in the spirit world. That is great sacrifice indeed.

"A deliberate termination of life, of one's own life is simply a lack of completion of that incarnation. If that which was intended to be learned has not been satisfactorily done, then that which is left undone will still need to be carried over to another lifetime, frequently picking up exactly the same difficulties that lead to deliberate termination.

"If the motive is to escape responsibility for one's deeds or to escape a situation that cannot be faced, then we say there will be counseling in the spirit world. If, however, the suicide attempt is as a result of sacrificing oneself out of love and consideration for another, this has the effect of reducing the loading against oneself. This, too, depends on the completion, successfully or otherwise of the program set before birth. Understanding is given according to the circumstances and the motives.

"We tell you that suicides are not regarded with any impatience by the spirit world, or with any judgment, for it is known that those who end their lives in this way will need to reincarnate and take up the same conditions again. They cannot escape those situations by ending one's life. With euthanasia, there is a difference in that one does not have to return to the same state of ill health. So if there is a difference, that is it. In both cases, there is much assistance given from the spirit world upon arrival there. Much care and attention and understanding are given to these souls."

Q. People who are seriously ill, and there are different types of people and how they deal with it. Negative people very often just give up and lose the will to live. Is that a form of suicide?

A. "The soul has a right to terminate its life by any means. It is its right to choose. If it has given up on this existence, then he/she in all probability will die if he has given up the will to live. However, this too must be faced, with compassion. We look upon these ones and gently point out to them the reasons why they did not need to give up. We treat them with kindness and understanding. We help them to see that the life need not have been so difficult that they could not endure it.

"This is again not a firm and rigid viewpoint, for there are those who have lived full and lengthy lives, who have achieved all that they could achieve and felt no purpose would be served by remaining. They are perfectly at liberty to decide to die. It is a different reason for giving up; it is a sense of completion, satisfaction, and readiness to depart. A different situation, I feel, from the one previous example."

Q. I am puzzled about suicides. A lot of people believe that there is an inner being that has close scrutiny, survey, and knowledge about our self and state of being. I would like to know whether or not that higher being can predict a state where one should take one's life, considering that we are for the most part living on a suicide trend by smoking, self-corruption, and bad living. We bear in mind a person who doesn't really intend to commit suicide but does after a call for help goes unheeded. It seems that the suicide could be clearer for me and others.

A. "It is quite clear. The guides, the inner self, and the soul self quite frequently bang at the door of the conscious mind that unfortunately does not always open that door. The ego mind is intent on acting independently. One might say it feels to have taken charge. It is this sense of being in control by the conscious self without paying heed to that which would save it that proceeds in a negative way to the extent of committing suicide. The soul self has done its utmost, has tried to call attention to the consequences, and has tried to aid in all ways.

"So many do not listen, so many are unaware, and they proceed irrespective of inner guidance. When that soul departs and leaves its physical body, the soul self is able to communicate better with its spirit guidance, and things are made clear. There is a period of adjustment as you are aware. Do not make the mistake of thinking that all souls are wise. They are not automatically wiser upon death. The soul too has a will and strength of will."

Q. Is the turnaround in such cases, between lifetimes that much quicker on account of unfinished business?

A. "It depends what you mean by length of turnaround. Time does not really have such great value. It is imperative for the development of the soul for onward progression to return and take up the thread yet again. However, the moment is to be chosen, the environment chosen, the correct parents chosen, all with care. The pattern must be set to enable a rectifying of that which has been darkened. It is not so much a question of length of time as a question of choosing the correct moment. This may be swift, and it may be lengthy. It depends on the understanding of the soul that requires adjustment and how quickly it comes to understanding and acceptance of what is required. There is no obligation. Understanding must come at its own pace and not be forced."

PURGATORY

Q. Is there such a thing as purgatory, as we are led to believe?

A. "It is yet another name that conjures up all sorts of visions of horror and hell. It is a place of spiritual cleansing according to the dictionary. We say that there is within each a possibility that they may be able to put themselves into a hell. But it would be of their own making. It is not a place that they are put into, for they put themselves into it. It is a state of being, a state of their own fears. It is what they create for themselves and is so often as a result of their belief system while incarnated and how they have conducted their lives. When they pass from physical matter, they carry with them perhaps remorse or fears. Whatever negative act they have condemned themselves for, they will still retain in their minds when they pass over, and this is their purgatory, though we do not like the word.

"They are still encapsulated in a world of their making. This does not mean that they will necessarily remain there. With time and counseling such as they will receive from helpers on this side will gradually bring them to an understanding of their state. They will work it out together with a trained wise counselor. It will be explained to them how they can change the existence of their own making. If they persist in striving to release themselves from their own fears and all that they have put around them, they will break free and be stronger as a result. They will have greater understanding. They in turn may choose to remain on that plane to assist yet others who come through in the same state."

I had occasion to deal with a spirit/ghost that was haunting a parsonage. When I tracked him down, it turned out to be a parson who had lived there. On talking to him, he told me he had preached hellfire and damnation during his life and had not behaved himself as he ought. Since his belief was strongly of hell and damnation, he was afraid to go to the other side. I could not convince him that it was otherwise. He is still there.

INTERLIFE

Q. How long before you come back after you die?

A. It varies. Nobody forces you to return. You make the decision yourself. A lot depends on how long it has taken to understand your actions and experience of the past life and to correct your thinking.

There is a lot of planning to do before you come back, and it is not just planning on your own account. You get counseling, to help you to decide what kind of life you wish to take on next time. You might need healing before you return. You might need to study so you can bring more expertise to the next life. You might need to wait until members of your family group return so you can plan a time together next time round.

You might plan to be born under a certain astrological sign so that you have the characteristics of that sign. You choose your parents and so might have to wait until they decide to have a child. You choose your environment and culture in order to understand another facet of being incarnated.

All this takes planning and waiting for the right moment in time. Some may wait years and years, and others could decide to come back almost straightaway.

Q. Is it always up to the individual when they incarnate?

A. As I have said, there is counseling, but yes, it is up to each to decide. If there is a continual resistance to reincarnating, then there is persuasion that it is in the best interests of the soul growth to go into a body again.

Q. Why don't we remember our former lives?

A. If you did that, you would be unlikely to be able to manage all the memories and could even be labelled schizophrenic as you tried to juggle them in your mind and behavior. Your mind would be so full of what went on before that you couldn't cope with it. It is hard enough to deal with current life situations, don't you think?

Q. So we are like a blank page each time we come?

A. Not exactly, because the quality of your soul and personality you have at birth is based on the lives you have had before. Each life helps you to be more than you were before. Nothing is lost to the soul memory and can be tapped into through meditation or past soul life regression. This is why it is so helpful to be able to do this and bring forward memory of those gifts that you have acquired through earlier incarnations.

You can enter into communication with your higher self through meditation, and that higher self will know just how much you can cope with in the way of information to help you. It won't give you anything you are not able to handle because it is working for your good. Meditation is the key to getting in touch with your helpers. Every single one of you has a helper or more.

Q. With respect to family members, do they link up after they pass on? Do they get together on the other side?

A. Oh yes, if they want to, and they do not always want to, as family members on earth do not always want to be together. You do not have to be with those you never want to meet again. In the majority of cases, the family members will reunite and be happy to do so. They will talk things over and decide what they want to do next.

All of us present different faces to the world. We are different at home to when we are at work, when we are at a party, when we are alone, and so on. We present our different faces in different situations and are assessed by others according to how we are dressed, how we speak, and whether we like this or that. Some use wealth to give them a position, some use guns, some emotional blackmail, and the many other ways used to be the person they wish to be. They find power in doing this, but the power is external. When they leave the body, they are seen for what they truly are, and there is no hiding one's true self. They have no trappings, they cannot use guns or position or wealth to get the power they want. If they are disagreeable, they cannot force somebody to be with them.

Q. I believe that people who pass over spend some time in some form of afterlife, before being reincarnated. If someone loses a loved one at a young age and then lives to old age themselves, will the loved one still be in the afterlife waiting to meet up again, or could they have been reincarnated as someone else so that the two miss each other? Or does time work differently between the different dimensions? Could the reincarnated one end up in a different soul group?

A. Since time is irrelevant in the spirit world and all things exist at the same time, any loved ones who have passed early will still be there for you, even if they have since reincarnated. Spirit consciousness is not limited by time or place and is everywhere and can manifest when and where it wishes. To prove this, at times your departed loved ones can still make themselves known to you on earth in spite of the different dimensions. Since you are not in physical third-dimensional form when you pass on to the fourth dimension after death, you can easily connect in a very real way with loved ones of the same vibration. You and they possibly being in separate soul groupings is irrelevant.

Q. Are there things that are punishable in the afterlife, i.e., sins?

A. There is nobody to punish you. There is no judgment from others, only understanding and compassion. Help is available to all who ask for it. This does not mean that you escape consequences of past sins. You alone with the help of spirit counselors work out how you can rectify and come to terms with what you have done. Sometimes what we regard as sins is not considered to be sins at all in the eyes of the spirit world. They may be regarded as errors of judgment due to inexperience. You are presented with your errors of judgment so that you and you alone can see what needs to be rectified in you.

Q. If the soul is neither male nor female and chooses to come back as either male or female, then are they disappointed when the body they choose is homosexual?

A. Frequently this occurs when one is undecided as to what it wants, as to what it wishes to be. Or simply to experience what it is to be both male and female in one form. For that was the original after all.

Q. What is the purpose for a child having a disability? What is the reason for this?

A. There are many variations here. A child who is born with a physical disability frequently has chosen that in order to either provide an opportunity for the parents to show love more strongly or to care for it in a different way to a child who was born healthy. Often there is an agreement between all parties that this would be the case. It also could be due to some karmic event, to compensate in some way for some act in the past. There are so many reasons why this takes place.

It is always desired by the soul and all parties in advance. Nothing happens by chance. This has been arranged to see if one can deal with the situation to the advantage of all or whether this is going to prove to be detrimental to the soul's purpose. It is a challenge, a learning experience.

Often a child's disability urges its parents to start a campaign to try to find a cure, so benefitting others besides themselves. Often a breakthrough is achieved, which could not have happened otherwise.

Frequently a physical form such as a baby that is damaged in some way has decided for the best possible reasons to allow the parents to learn something about themselves. There is a child in Japan who was born totally paralyzed. This child is a child of light. This child has learned at four years old to communicate messages from spirit and is now seen by thousands of people for the messages that he brings. This is a child who is paralyzed. You understand the gift that this child is bringing. He is an advanced soul, a bringer of light, and is touching not only his parents in a positive way, but also thousands. There is great advancement made by a child with a handicap of one kind or another.

Each of you has a goal to progress and not regress, to meet the changes that are occurring upon the planet, to meet challenges with a positive viewpoint, knowing that by doing this, you are advancing your soul. By seeing all situations in a positive light, even when they do not appear to be so, is assisting your soul's growth. You are here to be the best you can be and, by so doing, are inspiring others.

Q. Does the spirit world not have any control over man, because if a soul can choose to come back, why are some choosing to be scientists that can create things to destroy the earth? Why is that allowed?

A. A soul when it is born who decides to be a scientist usually has a thread where it has been scientifically focused in many lives, in that aspect of its soul. It is born generally with great plans in mind at a soul level for the ability to progress the nations through its scientific knowledge. Then it is born and is conditioned by its environment and situations that it meets. It is met with decision and choices, where frequently the choices are made in error. The spirit world does not have the right and is not able to change that decision.

"It is the right of every soul to make its own decisions to go this way or that way. We encourage right directions where we are given entry. We would assist if there were connection between us. If there was knowledge by these individuals that connection with spirit world was possible, then we could advise and counsel. We cannot change decisions; we can merely assist toward a better solution. Mankind must evolve through its own efforts, for if we were to block or stop things of that nature, then we are also preventing souls' ability to evolve.

"Having said all of that, when we see that the earth itself is being damaged by the actions of man, when the earth itself is in danger, then as a galactic force, we are able to influence sufficiently and to bring forces to bear that will rectify certain situations. We do this without interfering with choices of individual souls. We do this at another level. We do this at the level of vibrations and interactions with cosmic bodies. We do this by sending our own forces, our own evolved souls to earth to change opinions, to influence the minds, to influence but not to make decisions for others. We send waves of new arrivals to earth, often for the first time, of highly evolved beings that have abilities beyond the norm. There are many upon your planet at this time. Therefore, although man in many cases is bent on making decisions in error, to the detriment of others, there are many who are working for the good of man. We honor those who are incarnated on the earth for the challenges they face. We stand in awe of the courage shown in the face of adversity. We respect the feelings of those who suffer at the hands of others. The bravery that is shown by the mass of humankind is enough to evolve the human species to a much higher state of being. Do not dwell upon the negative aspects of your globe, for by so doing, you are reinforcing that energy."

RESISTANCE TO ILLNESS

Q. Would you say that those who have a strong immune system and do not catch diseases are free from fear? Is it possible to be completely resistant to epidemics?

A. "Yes, it is possible to be resistant to whatever force is around, whether they be epidemics or a minor passing through of illness or germ. It is possible. It is not frequent however. You will find there are those who suffer but appear to rejoice above their suffering and appear to be shining souls in spite of their suffering. These are ones who are meeting their challenges bravely and who have decided to meet their challenge in a spirit of shining light that will encourage others who also suffer in a like manner.

"We do not expect all strong positive shining souls to be trouble free, pain free, or ailment free, though it is indeed possible. Some of these shining souls have chosen deliberately to experience an illness. Perhaps, and quite frequently, provide a learning process for one dear to them so they may be near their loved one who is undergoing a learning experience and may encourage and assist on a close basis.

"Do not assess those who suffer as lacking in any soul intent. They may even be stronger than those who appear to be untrammeled by physical disabilities. There are those who attract many illnesses to them, allergic to this, that, and the other, to the atmosphere, etc. There is a wide range of reasons for this, dependent upon what they are reacting against. One needs to look at the particular aspect that causes distress to give a complete answer.

"Many times, troubles are inflicted upon them by circumstances around them, into which they have been drawn not of their own choosing. Too, you have those who do not intend to have any form of illness, of serious or mild condition, and their very belief in this is strong enough to keep them free of ailments."

TRANSPLANTING OF ORGANS

Q. Is transplanting of organs acceptable in the light of a soul's progress?

A. "If that soul is not to continue its existence incarnated, then it will reject the organ. If it has further work to do, then it will be a successful transplant. It is really quite simple."

Q. It seems that there is a lot of effort put in by medical staff and your world that is helping doctors to perform or to perfect techniques and scientific approaches to physical malfunctioning. Isn't there a purpose behind all that as well?

A. "The purpose is to develop within those specialized in medicine the ability to prolong life when it is required, when it is important that an individual continues to further its life's work. Indeed the experiences of near-death and then salvation by whatever means, be it a successful operation or transplant through the services of those experts trained to carry out the work is important. The experience of one such patient saved in this manner often is a trigger for that soul to assist others and provide support and love to those in similar situations. It brings a determination within that soul to assist others who might not otherwise continue with life. This in itself is of beneficial effect, a furthering of the spread of love of one to another."

EMBRYONIC STEM CELLS
sub title to Transplanting organs

Q. What is your view on embryonic stem cells?

A. "We in the spirit world do not view this as a bad thing except in one area. The cells taken are devoid of the soul. We applaud advancement that can give a better quality of life to any individual; for this is what this is about, is it not? Your physical form is given to you in order that you may interact with each other fully and learn how to love each other. It is purely a body, a form. It is not 'the total you.' The soul is the spirit that is in the body. There are many who choose to have certain ailments or physical disabilities deliberately to experience it so that they may have compassion for others later in a similar situation, or for a whole variety of reasons to do with their soul growth or the soul growth of another.

"That's one aspect, but then again, we applaud those who are attempting to assist those who suffer out of compassion of their hearts. This is what we are really saying except that there can be consequences of possible mismanagement. Once the ball gets rolling, it may be used in inadvisable ways, and this is what needs to be kept a watch on. There are many of you now who are living much longer. This is fine, but there needs to be some sort of control.

"So we would say we applaud those who are working to assist others in this way using stem cells. That is a very large generalization since there are other aspects to this. But who can point the finger at any one individual and say, 'Look, sorry, but you are not viable, so you must go.' You cannot do that, do you understand?

"There needs to be bigger spiritual understanding. You understand too that when we speak to you, we are speaking from different levels. We are speaking from a very detached viewpoint to some degree. We can see the bigger picture, and some of us speak as nonhuman beings and see the picture quite differently. As we are operating as one mind, we must take into account thoughts from different directions since we are not always in accord. It is not that one is right and one is wrong, it is simply that there are different aspects to be considered.

"The idea of stem cell research and usage was actually given to the human race from a nonhuman being. Now that should tell you something. The idea was given to you from the Arcturians. So you see, you have many helpers, and if you had been a child that had been saved through stem cell research, you would be applauding. You are all souls after all. We do not encourage cloning, although even that has two sides to it, for when you produce a body—cloned or otherwise—a soul will occupy that body, and so it is still another viable soul inhabiting a human body in much the same as if it had been conceived in the normal way.

NB: Arcturus

One of the twenty brightest stars in our galaxy. Said spiritually to hold enlightened beings. Also believed to be a portal for transfer of souls between lives. Many channelers receive information from Arcturians.

CHAPTER 6

SOUL

Q. I have heard it said that the soul resides in between the atoms of our body. Is that true?

A. "The soul does not reside between or among, it pervades the entire physical and etheric matter. It is in each and every atom, each and every space. It is within every minute part of your being. It is not residing between or in a particular spot. It is complete within and can remove itself on death."

SOUL GROUPS

Q. I have heard about soul groups and the idea that everyone influential in your life is part of your group throughout many lifetimes. Can you explain more about how this works? Specifically, if I have friends and family who are part of my soul group, but they also have countless friends and family of their own, are these others part of my soul group too, even if I don't know them? Or can you be part of more than one group?

A. There are different soul groups, and you can indeed belong to more than one. Some are family groups, and there are groups for joining with a common purpose and vibration. The group could be comprised of several souls or a few but who are all on your frequency. You might sense each other's presence in life and may find you want to come together.

Not all of your family or those within your acquaintances are connected with you as part of the soul group you belong to.

Family groups tend to reincarnate together, taking an exchange of roles with gender reversal and position within a family structure. This is to experience and perhaps sort out karmic lessons with the familiarity of each other. They will have shared many lives and experiences and wish to continue the relationships as different people. Soul mates can also be parents or children, friends, relatives, coworkers. It's always helpful to notice the dynamics that occur among family members.

There are lessons to be learned from the soul groups we choose to be a part of, good or bad, loving or hateful; they all exist for a purpose. Soul groups are not always easy since they can exist so that you are helped to deal with difficult issues with your own character or theirs. If these are not resolved, they may continue on to other lives until that part of you is corrected. Still, other soul groups have been together in lives where they had group experiences such as in persecution for religious beliefs or as in genocide (read about Cathars in *We Are One Another* by Arthur Guirdham).

Q. I understand that we arrive on planet Earth as spirit in human form and that members of our soul group also join us on Earth to fulfill certain tasks/lessons. Does this mean that we are unable to return to Earth in another body until everyone in our soul group has left their human bodies?

A. Not at all. You might easily reincarnate back into a soul group that is still on earth. Or you might simply rejoin just one member of that group. Groups do not always stay together in lifetimes but come together for special occasions. Members of the group come and go according to their own needs as well even when this does not include soul group members. Members of a soul group may also incarnate elsewhere in the universe if it serves a purpose.

SOUL GROWTH THROUGH FORGIVENESS

Q. I have a question on forgiveness and forgiving others. Please elaborate.

A. "Lack of forgiveness is a cause of many illnesses and is a handicap in itself. Where you find it difficult to forgive, you have not considered the self. You are constantly looking back to an action that is gone and not looking forward to see what can be made of the current situation that you are in. There may have been terrible deeds done to a soul that cannot forgive, and the effects of these deeds will continue for as long as they are held to in the mind.

"We are aware that one cannot always forget. We do not expect forgetfulness for what has happened. However, we ask that the injured one try to find some reason for actions that are so hard to be forgiven and so difficult to forget. Try to find some plausible reason that will bring about an understanding. Make excuses if you will, but above all, feel compassion for whoever has committed these unforgivable acts. Feel compassion for they are to reap the consequences in their future existence. You too if you do not forgive will reap the consequences of holding bitterness, for that bitterness will destroy you.

"You would be wise to detach and say, 'Well, that was difficult, and that was bad, and it hurt, but now I must go on. Now I must look to myself and see what I can make of what I have and not what was and try to see what I can make of what I am now.' They are hard lessons, and they do not come easily. But lessons they are, and you will be strengthened and rewarded in right treatment of your own being. For this is what you have to consider.

"And you have a bonus attached. The bonus is that you will be able to view others with compassion when you recognize similar conditions in them. You will be in a position to be of assistance through your own experience. So you will grow doubly, for you will be giving. If only you could realize how much you would benefit. The rewards are enormous."

Q. How may we put these words into action? How can we love all when there are vile deeds? How can we love one who has a black heart?

A. "We understand your dilemma, and we ask, if you are able, to seek an understanding of the deeds committed that appear so vile to you. We ask you to delve deeper than the superficial evidence that you see. In your probing, find a cause, not an excuse, but a cause.

KARMA

The universal law of cause and effect, or "as you sow so shall ye reap."

Q. Is karma real?

A. Karma arises from one's thoughts and deeds over lifetimes. Karma can be good or bad with relative consequences. Karma is not a system of punishment but is to teach us to learn to live in harmony. It is a learning experience whereby we gain wisdom.

Q. How do we clear past-life issues?

A. The simple answer is just to be the best you can be in any situation wherever you are and whoever you are with. That will clear and resolve any outstanding past-life issues. Don't try to drag them up and make too much of them. Your soul's purpose will have taken all that into account when deciding on your current life challenges. Trust your soul.

Q. When a person gets ill or has an accident, does it mean that they are in a karmic situation and that other people involved—i.e., family or friends—in this lifetime need to resolve matters in order for the situation to be healed, and if it doesn't get healed, then the situation will repeat until peace is made on the matter?

A. There are many reasons why things happen to people. When the same challenges are repeated over and over, it is simply because the need to address challenges have not been met. When you see what needs to be changed and viewed and reacted to differently, then there will be no more repeats. Not all accidents, illnesses, and so on are the result of karma.

Sometimes applying what happens to karmic causes can be a way of finding an excuse for not being responsible in this current life.

Q. Why are some people unable to recall their past lives? How can this be resolved? Also, why do we forget the lessons we have come back to learn when we are reborn? How can we learn our lessons and move on if there is no prompt? Surely, we could continue to reincarnate and unwittingly repeat the same mistakes over and over.

A. All that you have ever experienced and learned over your past lives make your soul what it is now with all its learning and errors. Whatever happens in your life may be similar to taking an exam over again. It would not do to give the answers before taking the test since there would be no real learning that way.

If you wish to have a prompt, then meditate and ask your guides or your soul consciousness for some clues. Remember that during the interlife, your past lives are discussed and you receive counseling and advice. By going into meditation your subconscious will assist in bringing this back to you.

Not all reincarnations are to learn how not to repeat mistakes but are simply to have fresh experiences. Mistakes are gifts so that you might grow more through understanding.

Does it help to know who you were? Yes and no. The point is you have had many incarnations, so you have been many things. Your past identity isn't as important as what you are here and now and what you can bring into this current time.

AKASHIC RECORDS

Q. What are the Akashic Records?

A. *Akasha* is a *Sanskrit* word meaning "sky" or "boundless space." The Akashic Records are said to be a collection of mystical knowledge that is stored on a nonphysical plane of existence. The Akashic Records are said to have existed since the beginning of the planet. Most writings refer to the Akashic Records in the area of human experience. The Akasha is said to be the library of all events and responses concerning the history of every soul since the dawn of Creation. Keepers of the Records is a name given to those who guard the Akashic Records. These are records of all souls and their journeys.

FEAR

Q. What is the best way to deal with fear?

A. "Fear comes from within yourself, and I am sure you know this already. What is it that you would fear? I will tell you how to deal with fear. First, have a belief system that nothing upon this earth or out of this dimension can harm you. It is only you that can harm yourself. There is self-preservation fear of course. If you were to have a vehicle sliding out of control toward you, you would naturally be fearful and do something to avoid a collision. That is self-preservation, but we are not speaking of this fear, are we? We are speaking of fear that arises from what you do not know. Fear of the unknown.

"The first step is to sincerely feel, believe and rest content in the knowledge that you are safe and secure, for it is only your soul that matters, not your physical form after all. Your soul continues, your physical form does not. We will give you an example. Think of your soul wearing an overcoat that is your body. If that coat were to be damaged, it would not create much disturbance in your mind. You would merely cast it off and replace it with another, for your soul would still be intact. It is how the soul reacts that is important."

Q. I have fear that is hidden. I am afraid I cannot release this fear. Is there a practical simple thing you can advise us to release ourselves from fear?

A. "Transform the word *fear* into something other. Replace the word *fear* with something less such as *experience*. Use a word that is not negative. Say to yourself, 'I am experiencing' not 'I fear.' Try not to put a negative aspect to it, and that will help you to enjoy the experience" (Metatron).

Ask for elements of the fear to be released in small steps through your dreams. Ask this before you go to sleep.

Q. This fear, how do we combat that, and how do we overcome that?

A. Fear comes about from the unknown. Recognize and acknowledge that you cannot be destroyed, that consciousness, your awareness continues. If you can recognize and accept that, no matter how others conduct themselves toward you, no matter what possessions you might lose or gain, no matter how you feel toward another. If you recognize that, then these things cannot damage you unless you allow it to affect your behavior. The main thing for you to realize and appreciate is that you are infinite and continual in existence.

"You have conducted yourself through many lives and are still here, are you not? Your awareness is still continuing. When you accept that, fear will vanish from you, for it will not matter if you are run over by a bus, it will not matter if a particular individual leaves you, if you are right within yourself.

"If you feel that your own conduct is to the best of your ability without intention of harm toward another, then you can be serene. If you have love within you, even for those who do not conduct themselves well toward you, you can rest serene. If you can still feel love, compassion, then you will have no fear in you.

"Your awareness does not disappear. You exist. You would exist even in a void. A negative, which fear is, is the opposite of love. Negative vibration simply cannot exist in a positive vibration. It would destroy itself or be transformed. Fear will be eliminated. It does not mean that you can walk out and step under a bus deliberately, for this would be foolish, would it not? You are not physically invincible. There is a difference. May I state the difference between fear and preservation? The self-preserving instinct has been coded into your physical form to ensure the survival of the species. It is not the same as fear of the unknown. There is nothing to fear except that which is in your mind."

Q. When negative energies attach to us, why does spirit not automatically detach them from us?

A. It is not the spirits' role to do our work for us. You can ask for their guidance, but the work is yours. If you are feeling secure in your own being, then nothing of a negative nature can attach itself to you. Dark cannot enter light without being transformed or destroyed. If you feel you have attachments, then look to see if there are any negative feelings in you. Most of what we see as attachments are our own fears. Others reading this may disagree with me, but I can only give you my own feelings on the matter. I personally have never had any dark energies attaching to me and so cannot speak from experience of that happening.

SPIRITUAL GROWTH

Q. Where and how does one develop spiritually? Is it in the earth life or in the spirit world, or is it a combination of the two?

A. "It is a good question. There is growth in all areas of existence. The greatest growth, the greatest understanding is through experience that you acquire on the earth or any other physical plane. Life is not easy on the physical plane where you have interaction with other souls who will act counter to your will, who will cause you pain, who will strive to have authority over you, or who will pamper you. Either way, the growth will come most from your physical and emotional experiences through interaction with other beings also in physical form.

"This is not to say that you must suffer to have spiritual growth. Growth is also achieved through compassion that is aroused in you when you see suffering and when you try to alleviate that suffering. Growth of your soul is achieved when you fight for right when you see a wrong. Growth is achieved when you exert yourself for the benefit of others. This does not entail suffering on your part, merely an arousal of your compassion and a desire to assist your fellow man. Growth is achieved when you exert your mind to benefit the world, whether in a small way or a large way. Growth is achieved when you are in communion with the Creator and when you absorb teachings to the point where they are put into action.

"It is on earth that you may put into action what is in your heart. It is difficult to put into action while you are in the spirit form only. Treat your existence here on this planet or any other planet as a great step forward for you, an opportunity to rise, to grow, and to raise your vibrations. We have many who sit and practice meditation and go through rituals to speed up vibrations to make themselves lighter. That is all well and good, but it is as nothing and does nothing to encourage spiritual growth if actions do not match this striving. You understand what I am saying.

"Many would like to become masters and high beings, without the work that is involved. By assisting others to understand, by being nonjudgmental, all those things that form part of spiritual law, that is what will achieve spiritual growth and greatness. That is what will raise your vibrations. You cannot go in by the back door. You have to earn a higher level. Those in the astral plane and above may not proceed to the higher vibrations until they have earned it. They have to be worthy before they are quite physically able to have their vibrations raised. It is a natural law, not one that can be bought or paid for or achieved in any other way. There is no back door. Only by your deeds, your thoughts, actions, and your compassion for others can you rise up."

Q. What is the purpose of our emotions?

A. There are many worlds without any emotion, and they feel the lack of it for they feel incomplete. Our emotions help us to feel compassion and love for others. Emotion helps us to know right from wrong so that we might grow spiritually. Emotion helps us to feel really alive; without it, we would be no more than robots. Emotion enables us to appreciate the wonders of the world in which we live and the music and arts that have been produced by emotional individuals. Emotions stir us into action when we see injustice.

Q. I wonder what the point of humanity is, as I can see eventually we will destroy our Earth, so what is the reason for our existence?

A. By humanity, I assume you mean the human race. The human species was developed to give souls a wonderful opportunity to grow and develop on a most beautiful planet having an amazing diversity of species, geographic, and climatic conditions. It was and still is a fabulous option to choose from a whole range of environments one would like to experience. There are many queuing up to take advantage of incarnating on this planet. The planet Earth will not be destroyed by the human race. It is the university of life where souls can grow at the fastest pace.

Q. Everyone is spiritual as we know it, but can a person be spiritually declining as much as evolving?

A. If a person persists in conducting the life contrary to spiritual law and ethics in spite of counseling during the interlife, then the soul can be retrograde. If a person indulges in black energies such as negative voodoo, then it is likely to harm its soul.

NB: **Voodoo**—a primitive religion of West African origin found these days also with Haitians, West Indians, and with some natives of Southern United States and South America. It is a belief in sorcery, witchcraft, and the use of fetishes and charms.

Q. Can your spiritual level get higher by traveling to Peru, Egypt, or other powerful areas on this planet?

A. Your spiritual level is totally dependent on the way you conduct your life wherever you are. Being in areas of high powerful energies enhance your own energies and may make it easier to meditate and raise your vibrations. Therefore, it is beneficial by aiding you to make contact with the spirit world that might help you to conduct your life well. But you alone are responsible for your spiritual level.

Q. Is there something like "the right path"?

A. Whatever path you are on is the right one since there are no wrong paths. Even if it feels as if things are going wrong and not as you would wish, then this is the right path for you. This is because when things go wrong, it gives you the chance to grow by getting things right in spite of the difficulties or disappointments. View what you might think as a wrong path as an interesting journey with new and exciting things to learn. If all is going the way you would wish and you can "feel" it is so, then it is evidence that you have got it right and can move forward in the way you have chosen.

CHAPTER 7

OUR ORIGIN

Q. Planet Earth is packed full with life-forms—in the air, on the land, and in the seas. Is it really true that we all arrived from single cells living in the water? If so, why have so many different life-forms evolved from the same single cells, some of which are said to have arrived at the start in perfect form and have not needed to evolve at all, i.e., sharks, crocodiles?

A. The Earth was seeded and encouraged to develop through the evolutionary process. This diversified forms so that they were viable during the many changes that Earth has undergone throughout its history. Therefore Darwin's theory of evolution is correct to a certain point in our journey. Then more visitors arrived from other planetary systems merging and developing that which they found to be attractive and likely to be suitable for advanced civilization. I have no information on sharks or crocodiles. Earth is considered by the galactic family to be a seed star. There have been many seeded civilizations from star systems that have now left Earth.

Q. Do we as spirit have to start as single cells and in time work up through being animals etc. to having a human body?

A. All life has spirit in it, not all life has a soul. Spirit can enter *as a soul* directly into human form according to its level of growth, irrespective of the physical development of a facet of nature. It is known that in the very early stages of embryonic development, we resemble identical features of animals.

Q. During life on Earth, all creatures appear to have parasites living on them, also, bugs like flu, etc. Are these smaller beings a type of alien life force come to take over planet Earth?

A. Bugs, parasites, microscopic bacteria, and so on are all part of the food chain, which is necessary for life on a larger scale. They have not come to take over the Earth but are absolutely vital to its health.

Q. How did we begin as human beings? How were we created?

A. "You were created by mind, by an intelligence, as was the universe. That is how the world was made—by thought, by an intelligence." Darwin was correct in his evolution theory up to the point of the apes. Then we were visited by interplanetary visitors and celestial sons who interacted and interbred with these animals, deliberately genetically altering them so as to bring a highly developed civilization into being on Earth.

Q. In my spiritual search so far I believe that we are all from the "stars" originally, I think I may be from Sirius or Orion! However, we are also "from"/are God, does this mean we have lived as spiritual or physical entities on different planets or stars once we were "born" from God, and before we have incarnated on earth? (From Cara Wade.)

A. The universe and other star systems, including Orion and Sirius, are all part of the Creation we call God. As such, they too have a spiritual aspect with their own physical and spirit world. Most of us here on Earth have begun our soul journeys on other planets in various forms and have come to Earth to inhabit and develop on such a wondrous planet.

I believe that humanity was seeded on Earth by advanced civilizations in the cosmos. Some believe the DNA of some primate-type species was altered to produce *Homo sapiens*—we may be an experiment and left to our own devices to be studied in much the same way that scientists might watch animals.

We were created to help us evolve into higher spiritual beings and one day also become enlightened enough to join the galactic community.

ANGELIC REALM

Q. Where and what is meant by the angelic realm?

A. It is where angels are said to live, each according to their order and mission. This is not a physical place or area but a division in the imagination. *Realm* in this case refers to an area of jurisdiction and care for mortals by angelic forces. There is a vast order of angels who are located in their respective order of work.

Metatron is the highest of the angels. The hierarchies evolve around the programs of divine authority expressed through the high command of Metatron, Michael, and Uriel operating with the diety absolutes of Gabriel, Raphael, Ariel, and the Creative forms of the Holy Spirit, Shechinah in diety trinitization. Gabriel said he was his brother. Lords of light Metatron, Melchizedek, and Maitreya. And "only Metatron can take you into the presence of the Divine Father."

Q. Is it possible to channel the angelic realm?

A. Of course it is. Angels frequently make connection with aspiring souls. However, they are not usually very vocal or wordy. It is more to do with feeling their presence. You can channel their energy and thoughts.

Q. Angels are said to be neither male nor female, as there are a number of humans at this point in time who are happy to have same-sex relationships, is this part of the human race, changing over to a new frequency of energy where being either male or female is no longer required?

A. How angels are seen is according to the one doing the seeing. Some are male and some female and some androgynous. They present themselves as they wish to be seen in any form. Those humans who have both male and female tendencies had decided to do so before incarnation, or were undecided when making their plans for life.

Q. Are there angels on our planet?

A. If you suspect somebody to be an angel and ask, "Are you an angel?" would they tell you whether they are or not? They would probably smile sweetly and say, "What do you think?" (*Laughter.*)

Can you imagine if they were to go round saying, "I am an angel," they would not be taken seriously. You can recognize an angel by their glow, by their positive outlook, by the way they treat those around them. Even if you are walking in a crowded street and one comes toward you, there is oftentimes something about that individual that helps you to recognize that it is a special being, without even passing a word. There are those that carry a glow with them in the darkest of places.

Angels can appear in human form when assistance is required and asked for at times of great need. There are many stories to this effect. So yes, there are angels on this planet.

Q. The concept of an angelic being is one that appears in many religions—each of which has similarities and yet also contains many differences. For example, Tantric Tibetan Buddhism has very clear views on angels, which they refer to as *daka* and *dakini* (yes, they have female angels), but while they regard the angelic hordes as beings of good, they also regard them as having very little if any patience and as entities not to be trifled with—they have an almost-abject terror of them. What are they, how do they come about, and how is this remarkable contrast in the way they are perceived possible?

A. Except for the well-known archangels, angels of past times have been given names and conceived of in a variety of ways. A Lakota spiritual teacher said, "What Christians call angels we call spirits." It may be believed that when an angel was seen in the past, what was actually seen was in fact an extraterrestrial. Many subscribe to the view that some seen as angels come from space and may appear fearsome and forbidding. Many extraterrestrials have wings or appear apparently from nowhere and would come with the light surrounding them according to their mode of travel.

SPIRITUAL REALMS

Q. What exactly is a spiritual realm, and where is it?

A. It is said to be an undefined area where discarnate beings exist and where the highest spiritual values are held.

ASCENDED MASTERS

Q. Who are the Ascended Masters?

A. They are spiritual beings who have risen in their vibrations through incarnation experiences and so have ascended to a higher plane of consciousness, i.e., closer to the Divine. When a Master such as Jesus as the Christ Michael, or any of the great ones, show themselves either in the mind or physically, they will demonstrate their form so as to be recognized, that is to say they will wear the robes, they will maintain the imagery that mankind has given them so that they might be recognized as who they are, but in truth, they are much more than that.

For how else would they be able to manifest to the human mind? The human mind is not capable, or cannot withstand, the fullness of their glory. We are sure many have had Jesus speaking to them often to great effect. It is his essence that is everywhere at all times. When you communicate, it is your essence that has reached out to him, and there is a union, a connection made. It is glorious.

The Ascended Masters are also known as the White Brotherhood or Celestial Sons or the Communicators. (See book *Being Human*.) Their role is to work with the planet Earth and its inhabitants.

CELESTIAL SONS

Those said to be colaborers and cocreators with the Maker, chosen to assist with the evolutionary process and spiritual progression of Earth forms. Later often referred to as the White Brotherhood.

Q. What is the Great White Brotherhood?

A. They are a group of Ascended Masters whose objective is to assist Earth and humanity in spiritual evolution. This group is the same as the **White Brotherhood**. It is referred to by both titles according to how one feels at the time of reference. *White* refers to purity, not color.

Q. Who are the Masters?

A. These are souls who have had incarnations on earth who have spiritually advanced to a high degree. This has enabled them to go to the higher dimensions where they work for the benefit of mankind. A Master Soul is the soul of one who has attained a high spiritual status through a succession of incarnations.

Q. Who is it that communicates with us when channeling?

A. "We are collectively known as the Teachers. We may or may not introduce ourselves when we come as we prefer to be known collectively."

Melchizedek

In Old Testament history, meaning "a priest." Melchizedek is an exalted patriarch as principal angel and future ideal figure. In modern thought, he is one who has passed through many levels of consciousness retaining memory of each.

Q. I was particularly interested in Melchizedek. Can you tell us any more about them?

A. Well, what would you like to know about Melchizedek? They are a very high order of beings, very high indeed. For any soul to have reached all those levels and have conscious knowledge of it is extreme advancement. The Melchizedeks are known as the Emergency Sons who incarnate on planet Earth on a temporary basis.

Machiventa Melchizedek was one who did this and lived and taught at Salem two thousand years before Christ. He was a wise teacher to many religions over the world and has an order of Melchizedek missionaries who carry on his teachings.

Q. Would they ever reincarnate into our being?

A. Yes and no. If Melchizedek decided to be in physical form on the planet Earth, there is more than one way that he might do it. The main method is to take—ah, to exchange bodies.

There are many references to Melchizedek as an enigmatic figure twice mentioned in the *Hebrew Bible*, also known as the *Old Testament*. Melchizedek is mentioned as the king of Salem, and priest of God Most High in the time of the biblical patriarch *Abram*. He brought out bread and wine, blessed Abram, and *received tithes—from him*, (*Genesis 14:18-20*). Reference is made to him in *Psalm 110:4* where the victorious ruler is declared to be "priest forever after the order of Melchizedek."

DIFFERENT CONSCIOUSNESS

Fields of Consciousness

Q. What is consciousness?

A. Consciousness is not limited by space or time. It is a field relating to all thoughts, ideas, emotions, and mind workings that have existed and continue to exist for all time. It may be tapped into by intent in much the same way as a radio is tuned until the desired station is achieved. The various fields refer to the scope of innumerable subjects that exist.

God Consciousness

An awareness of a god force. A knowing that we are all part of this god force and are not separate from it.

Greater Consciousness

A mind that is greater than our own and which covers a wider range than we do.

Great Subconscious

The knowing or wider range of consciousness that is beneath or hidden from our conscious mind until we delve into it.

Higher Realms of Consciousness

Areas of consciousness where the highest values are held, relating to purity, truth, clarity, and love. This is where evolved spiritual beings reside.

Higher Forces

Powerful spiritual forces that work only for the good of all creation.

High Spiritual Beings

Q. Who would you say were high spiritual beings?

A. Clearly there are spirits superior in evolution to lower-plane entities. One would class Jesus or Melchizedek as a high spiritual being in contrast to those who are still on the early rungs of spiritual development or have just departed the third dimension. Generally those who have achieved high spiritual values through their own evolutionary process are regarded as high spiritual being.

WHAT IS ASCENSION?

Q. Is there a hierarchy in the spirit world? Do we evolve as we go on?

A. Great spirits conceive of themselves as being equal with others. However, there is, I believe, a hierarchy among the celestial hosts. It is to be hoped that we will and do evolve as we proceed through our incarnations. That is the objective.

Q. Is there a leader such as in an organization on the other side?

A. That is a difficult one to answer correctly. They tend to consider themselves equal and of one mind. They are put into categories according to their skills and abilities in handling certain needs. Maybe the sections are based on spiritual growth, scientific healing, or artistic learning and so on. All have a natural field of interest. We are all aware of the various angels and saints called upon for a variety of needs, such as St. Christopher for travel, St. Anthony to find lost things.

Q. Is the world population really going into the fourth and fifth dimension by 2012?

A. It is to be hoped, but whatever you do while in this life will carry you forward into the next dimension and create a good, or not-so-good for some, existence. The planet will not die. Concentrate on your own growth.

Q. As we enter into the fifth dimension, will we see higher-dimensional colors?

Will we immediately be more telepathic, or will this be a more gradual occurrence?

A. It is frequently said by those who have ventured into the fifth dimension that colors are brighter there than anything we can conceive of here. The ability to use telepathy is being increased even in the third dimension so that there will not be quite such a dramatic change later. For some it will take some time to adjust to simply "knowing" what is being imparted. For others it will occur quite naturally.

OTHER WORLD LIFE—LIFE ON THE OTHER SIDE

Q. What is it like in your spirit world? (Addressed to a guide.)

A. "My world is as I wish it to be. I could if I wish take it very easily, but it would not help me. I would become as stagnant in this world as those who do nothing for their growth in your world become stagnant. Stagnation means decay; therefore, I prefer to utilize what is within me and exercise it for the growth of souls. This naturally adds to the growth of my own soul and the group soul. It is therefore to my own benefit that I do not take what you would term a lazy existence.

"I can discourse with many similar beings and exercise my thought processes. I can, and many do, visit those who are troubled and on certain levels less advanced, those who have not yet reached a fuller understanding of life here. I can visit, help, and encourage them, though I cannot do their work for them. I can merely ease their troubled thoughts and bring them to a greater understanding.

"We have places of care and attention for those who require it. We have areas where one can visit for debates on intellectual matters in whatever field is of interest, where we can decide on how best to pass on our knowledge for the benefit of those who need it. We can, and I say *we*, for we do not all choose the same area of work, we can work with those souls yet to be reborn and discuss with them their preferences for their next existence. Our world is very much an area of thought. Thought is action. It is an energy that is real. It is vital.

"We have areas that attempt to nullify black thoughts that still come from some souls, even on our plane. You find this surprising. It is so. We too even here must have balance and must test ourselves against forces that would delay us and turn us back. We must test our mettle and prove our worth, for if we are not worthy, how can we progress? How can we assist if we do not prove our own worth and knowledge and experience at all levels? It is good that we do not wish to stagnate as there is a long way for us to go yet."

CHAPTER 8

WALK-INS

Q. What is a "walk-in"?

A. It is generally understood that a "walk-in" is a soul that has evolved sufficiently to be allowed to exchange places with an already incarnated person in order to carry out a mission. In this way, it does not have to go through the birth process or early childhood where it could be distracted or adversely influenced by those early years. Walk-ins are beings who have attained sufficient awareness of life allowing them to forgo the process of birth and childhood (see Ruth Montgomery's books *Strangers among Us and Threshold to Tomorrow*). When a new soul comes into physical embodiment through the walk-in process, the original soul normally leaves. The incoming soul assumes full responsibility, and before it gets on with its mission, it cleans up any mess that the outgoing soul may have left behind.

Q. Isn't this possession?

A. No. **A walk-in can only take place with full agreement of both outgoing and incoming souls**. In most cases, the person is not consciously aware of the soul exchange since the incoming soul inherits the cellular memory of the physical body. Its new human life often continues in a relatively seamless manner.

Q. Why would a soul want to leave before its time?

A. There are many reasons why a soul departs early. It could be due to a long illness or a sudden accident. Or there can be a feeling that they want to quit life, finding it too hard but lack the courage to commit suicide. How often have you heard of someone who survives a terminal illness, a near-death experience, or who has had a miraculous escape from a near-fateful accident and then has a new lease of life and goes on to raise funds or provide inspiration in one way or another? Often they seem to be a changed person in more ways than one to those who knew him or her.

Q. What happens to the outgoing soul?

A. It moves on to other experiences in nonphysical worlds and reincarnates when it is ready, just as it would if it had gone through a physical death.

Q. Is it possible for a soul to swap a body with another soul partly through life?

A. "Yes, it is done frequently. When a soul has decided and desires to depart but does not want to physically die, then an agreement is made with a soul wishing to enter without going through the birth process. Generally, these souls have made an agreement well in advance, even though the physically incarnated soul does not remember. When life has become untenable for an individual, then may a soul who has a purpose in life and mission to accomplish and who is evolved enough not to go through the birth process, then it may enter, and the soul wishing to depart may do so. There is a contract that is made. The incoming soul agrees to clear up any mess the departing soul may have left. That is the agreement. We are talking about a mess in this particular lifetime, not karmic debts. Karmic debts always belong to the soul and not to the physical body.

"The incoming soul takes on the cellular memory of the body. Each cell of the body holds memory of that lifetime. It is not resident in the brain organ alone. In this way, the incoming soul has total recall of everything that has happened to that body since birth. Frequently, upon entry and for some time after, it does not remember that it is an incomer. To the family or friends, it appears as if nothing has changed except perhaps for a change of personality or a new drive. It sometimes takes two years to relate to the new life and the new body and begin the mission it has set out to accomplish. We call these walk-ins. These entries are only allowed when approved of by a higher council. It has to be shown that the walk-in has a sufficiently worthwhile mission to be allowed to do this and is adequately evolved to carry out its task. There is no karmic debt incurred by the soul for having departed early. It simply ends this life earlier and then carries on, as normal, in the normal cycle of life and death. Each soul has infinity in which to develop and arrive at some particular point. There is no hurry. It is not essential to complete each lifetime as there are many more to be had."

Q. What happens if someone remembers past lives but is a walk-in? Who does the past life belong to?

A. Past-life recall always belongs to the soul and not the body; although the body that the incoming soul has taken on may show physical evidence of past lives belonging to the outgoing soul.

MYTHICAL BEASTS

Q. Question regarding the existence of mythical beasts on planet Earth.

A. "Excellent question, for they all existed. All of them have existed on your planet, and indeed, when you speak of the little people such as fairies and elves and pixies, they still exist, they are still on your planet. They are still here, they have always been here. It is simply that you cannot see them in much the same way as you cannot hear the music that we make. Dragons, yes indeed, they existed. Giants, they existed. They have all taken place on your planet, and this is where you get the mythological stories about them for they have been on Earth. If you take the concept that you can travel through time or are able through your meditations to travel through time, you may with intent meet these creatures. If you are traveling through time, they still exist in their time when they were actually physical on your Earth. All it takes is for you to travel to that period to be able to meet them, if that is your desire.

"You understand that all matter has intelligence. Even each single cell has intelligence, for it knows where it belongs and will hasten to group with other cells similar to its own, for its intelligence tells it to. For example, intelligence within your body directs assistance from certain cells to the site of a wound. It is a different intelligence to that of soul consciousness. It is an instinctive natural thing, genetic. One might say it is intelligent design.

"Life upon your planet is so varied; it is a marvel in itself. One only has to study nature to understand and wonder at it."

HALLUCINOGENICS

Q. Can we use hallucinogenic drugs to help us raise our level of spirituality?

A. This can be dangerous, and your level of spirituality is dependent on your conduct throughout life, not on drugs, which may open you psychically but not spiritually.

Some have ventured to take ayahuasca, often called the vine of the soul. It is a hallucinogenic plant from the Amazonia rain forest used and concocted by shamans to obtain visions through trance and by leaving the body. This is not advisable for those who have no experience of the spirit world and who are fainthearted. It is not a pleasant experience and should only be taken with others accustomed to the practice, preferably shamans of the Amazon who are able to monitor and assist during the process. It is not addictive fortunately.

CHAKRAS (including all the different chakras and their locations)

Q. How much should we know about chakras?

A. Chakras are the energy centers of the body, both physical and spiritual. There are seven main ones aligned with the spine, with others at various points of the body, some extending beyond the physical form. When seen by clairvoyants, healers, and the like, they appear to spin. The word *chakra* comes from Sanskrit, meaning "wheel."

Starting from the base, the first chakra is red and is situated at the genitals. This is used for energy, passion, and as grounding.

The second one, colored orange, is called the sacral chakra and placed just below the navel.

Above that at the solar plexus, it is yellow. The fourth is green or pink and is known as the heart chakra. Then at the throat, it is turquoise. This relates to the communication center. The brow chakra or known as the third eye is in indigo blue and is placed between the eyes just above the brows. Next is the crown chakra, violet. This center opens to receive the energy of the great cosmic consciousness.

There are others as I have said but are too numerous to mention here. All chakras have a connection with parts of the body, and health may be influenced in rebalancing by use of crystals, pendulums, and healing hands.

Q. The healing energy of Reiki or universal energy—can this energy last forever, or can this energy be tired as well, as the magnetic field of planet earth has declined?

A. Universal energy lasts forever and will not diminish. It is not only magnetic energy. There are many forms of energy, and these can change. We do not yet know all forms that exist.

DNA CHANGES

Q. Would you speak about the DNA changes that are said to be happening?

A. "There is adaptation being made by those who are serving others to bring a higher understanding to the populations on the Earth, to bring them a desire to know. It is like prodding them with a little stick to wake them up. Changes are being introduced into the DNA not only to those who are spiritually minded but also to the entire race of humankind. It will be unnoticed. It will not be recognized. It will be gradual since to do it any other way could be harmful."

Q. Would you explain any physical changes that may occur or which are occurring in these times? I am having a lot of mucus, which I never had before.

A. "As a result of the changing wavelengths from planets and the sun, there are differing energies affecting Earth and people. This is similar to the way the moon not only affects the tides but also the rhythm of cycles within people. There is currently a lot of attraction and pulling from various planets. Because you are a water-based system, the tides within your body and emotions will be affected. This has also to do with a planetary body that is entering your solar system in this period of time. This is affecting all manner of things."

"In addition, there is genetic engineering on many on your planet, taking place in order to elevate the physical form. That is to say to enable it to survive differing conditions that may or may not occur in your future. Adaptations are being made similar to those with the DNA. This is to ensure the survival of the human race.

"We cannot rely on the pace of evolution to do this, for things are moving too quickly, so we are making adjustments. If you feel tired when you should not, or have sudden bursts of energy and can't understand that, or excessive mucus, these are signs. We tell you that excessive mucus is also due to your atmosphere, to the chemicals that are not only in the food chain but also in the air and water. You cannot avoid this now for it is into everything. That too is making changes in the physical form, which is why we are helping to alleviate that by helping you to adjust."

PINEAL GLAND

Q. Would you talk about activating the pineal gland please?

A. Well, the pineal gland is already active, else you would not be functioning as a human being. It affects many parts of your body already. What you are asking is when will it be activated even more? It is related to inner sight, the third eye, and awakening. It is also the body's biological clock, which regulates and monitors electromagnetic fields. Therefore, when the electromagnetic (EM) wavelengths start to affect Earth, it also produces change in the pineal gland, which has been called the gateway to the soul. A change in the Earth's magnetic field can trigger a psychic awakening through the effect this has on the pineal gland.

This gland is related to opening the Kundalini, which if activated too quickly can be dangerous. So briefly, the pineal gland will be more in use but in gradual stages to see how it goes with the current human being. You also have the pituitary gland that affects the hormones.

PEACE

Q. Will there ever be peace among us?

A. "What you feel today will influence your future. If you desire peace, if incarnated souls desire peace, if the aggressive element is weeded out from the DNA, you will have peace. We tell you that the aggressive nature of mankind has been brought to your planet from a race from another system and has bred itself into the human species. This is what we are trying to eliminate."

Q. Where did they (this race) come from?

A. "There was more than one, but we do not wish to pass judgments on other systems. There are others, but if we tell you who, they will forever remain in your mind as the baddies. This does not help. When focus is on the negative, then that will be your future. Set your mind in the direction of greatness. What your mind focuses on, where the attention goes, that is what will grow. Set your mind to greatness; fill your hearts with love. We know this is not easy when there are so many unlovable happenings on your planet. When you hear or view terrible happenings, terrible actions, if you view the souls that are bringing this about as extremely unhappy distorted souls, remember that infinity will be their lot. Know that they will have retribution and will in turn suffer, and then perhaps you can find compassion in your hearts for a soul that is suffering. Compassion is akin to love, is it not? When you send compassion to a wrongdoer at whatever level, then you are already changing things for the better.

"Try to be forgiving, try to be understanding, for in your turn, you have been there and have come through and are now thinking in different ways. You have, each of you in past lives, been where these others are now. They are merely walking their way through to their higher states. Try to feel compassion for them. You see, it is easy to love the loveable, is it not? It is not so easy to love the unlovable. You don't have to like them, you know, but find compassion."

CHAPTER 9

OTHER WORLDS

EXTRATERRESTRIAL INTELLIGENCE

Intelligent beings—physical or otherwise—that are not of the planet Earth.

Q. Is it possible to channel an extraterrestrial?

A. "Of course. Many channeling through now are from another planetary system. It is for this reason that we must use telepathy, for you would not understand the language. It could not be interpreted if it were brought through in our language or sound. However, we do this at times to selected individuals. (I receive and speak in several of their languages and understand the sense of what they wish to say. We have conversations.)

"This does not mean that those from other planetary systems do not communicate with you in other ways. It is not always recognized as such, but the information indicates where we are, where we come from, or what our purpose is. Our purpose has a far wider reach than those (guides) teaching you as individuals for your own personal growth. This is a much wider area of concern and interest. It encompasses your planet, your solar system, and the future of other worlds. This is how you will know when you are in contact with someone from another planet. The information comes with a different slant and emphasis.

"We are able to speak in our own language, which has an effect on those present at all times. It has a vibration that has a beneficial effect on physical matter, the brain cells, the heart; and that in itself creates an awakening. Therefore, it is beneficial when we speak to you in our sound. It will not harm you, for we are not taking all this effort to harm you."

Q. Has Sirius got a role to play?

A. "Oh absolutely, it has always. It is a star system that is gravitationally connected with planet Earth. Sirius is responsible to a major degree for the existence of the human race. So yes indeed, it has a strong connection. It is linked gravitationally with the planet Earth, so it cannot help but have an interest. Many of the beings on your planet have come from Sirius. They are the by-products, if you like, of the significant others, as we have been called. For it is because of those from Sirius and a group of planetary systems, Sirius being the leader of the pack, that your planet Earth has been saved more than once from destruction.

"It is their interaction on your behalf with those in much higher authority that the planet Earth be saved, for it has great value. You understand that many of your so-called gods of the past have come from Sirius in the early days, when they were first interacting and developing the human species, which is why in your ancient cultures such as your Native Americans and Mexicans, Africans, all the old races, have such strong connection with those from Sirius, with the bird-tribe. This is why their dancing, powwow, and ritual dance ceremonies use bird-head masks. They are not representing birds as creatures from Earth so much as representing visitors from Sirius. They are still attempting to assist you to a very large degree.

Q. What is the difference between Sirius A and Sirius B?

A. Sirius is a large binary star system consisting of a bright white star named Sirius A and a faint white dwarf companion named Sirius B. Sirius B is invisible to the naked eye but packs almost the entire mass of our sun into a globe only four times as large as the Earth. Sirius B's surface is three hundred times harder than diamonds, while its interior has a density three thousand times that of diamonds. Spinning on its axis about twenty-three times a minute, it generates huge magnetic fields around it. It has been suggested that there is also a third star in this system, namely Sirius C. Sirius B is where your dolphins came from, for they are souls and chose to come to Earth because it too is a water planet, as are some other planetary systems. There are planets around both that have not yet been recognized or seen by your scientists. They have not been able to detect them. So the relationship is close, obviously, in much the same way as the Earth's relationship with Mars and Venus is close being in orbit round the sun."

Q. Regarding Sirius B, you said that the dolphins that come to our planet have souls. What is the difference between a soul that is human that has come from Sirius B and the actual dolphin?

A. "The souls are all the same. There is progression of souls, by that we mean advancement. Earth beings at the moment are advancing souls. We are all learning to progress to a higher state, to be closer to the Divine Source, and that is true of all souls. Whether the souls inhabit a form that is not human, whether it be a dog or a dolphin or an elephant or whatever, or any creature on another planet, they are all souls, and they are all in their own level of progression.

"The souls of those who are dolphins have progressed much more rapidly. They have progressed along a dissimilar path to your technology. Their intention was to develop alongside a direction involving the planet Earth. We are talking about spiritual advancement here, but all souls hopefully are attempting to advance themselves toward a Divine Source. That is the purpose of a soul, whatever form they take up.
"A dolphin's soul between incarnations as a dolphin, and remember it is an intelligent force, even if it is simply an orb such as is taking place these days and being seen these days. It may decide to incarnate as a human being just for the experience. So you could have a soul that has been a dolphin incarnating as a human being."

Q. Are there any other planets that have as much conflict as we've got?

A. "Yes, there have indeed been other planets that have gone through what you are going through now, and they have come through. They are now on a (pause)—we were going to say a straight path, but that is not possible, is it? But you understand me; they have come through and are continuing. We tell you that there are uncountable numbers of planets that have intelligence and growth such as you have on the planet Earth. You are not alone. You will never ever be alone. Some who are now attempting to assist you have been on these planets where disaster has struck, so they understand fully how it is for you."

CROP CIRCLES

Q. Here is my question: Is there a spiritual meaning to crop circles' appearance? Do these crop circles come from a togetherness-consciousness or are really made from other dimensions or identities or spirits that produce these?

A. Most recognize that not all crop circles are manmade. In fact, only a few are, and it is clear which of these come into that category. However, there are large numbers that are created by space visitors with messages to our planet. I have been told by spirit that it will be scientists who decipher what their meanings are. It will be the researchers and people with advanced degrees in science and engineering. They seem to be symbolic messages from an unknown, high intelligence. The evidence supports the theory that human beings could not have made so many of the thousands of crop circles worldwide.

LIFE ON OTHER PLANETS

Q. I speak of the entire universe from one vast end to the other—not just our own Milky Way. The question I pose is "Are there universe(s) other than our own . . . perhaps even in other dimensions? If so, who created them?" (Basil, Florida)

A. There are uncountable universes other than our own. All that exists was created and is still being created by a great intelligence, The Creator of all things that are involved with existence. That is, we are the intelligent design; we are part of it and so are not separate. There are parallel universes and many dimensions all operating simultaneously.

Q. Given that the universe is greater than our vision or understanding will allow, how so that we allow our perspectives of limitation to prosper? Do we not acknowledge that there are other worlds and other vistas ever present? The question so is, do our spiritual guides and teachers acknowledge hidden worlds and peoples of the stars?

A. Of course, they do.

Q. In your world, do you age quicker than we do in our world?

A. We don't think about age. We leave when we feel like it. Age doesn't come into it.

Q. Do you stay one age, do you stay, say, thirty or forty years of age?

A. No, we're speaking more like several hundred years. But we decide when we've had enough.

Q. And which dimension do you go into?

A. "That is like saying how many leaves are there in a tree? For each individual, as they do on planet Earth, it is according to our own level of attainment of awareness."

Q. You don't grow like we do, we age and grow wrinkly and slow down?

A. "We have rejuvenation processes. It's all to do with the mind, of course. You on Earth have told yourselves that you age physically as you grow older in years, and so you do. If you told yourself otherwise, then you would not. It's as simple as that."

Q. In your world, you don't obviously—don't have ailments like Alzheimer's or anything like that or where people have bad hips or bad legs?

A. "Oh, indeed we do, we have ailments, but they are quickly repaired. Ailments always come from the mind and not visited on us as they are in your world, via chemicals that are not suitable for the body."

Q. Do we do more damage to ourselves from our own mind?

A. Indeed, but there are also outside influences as we have said. But you know, if your mind was strong and focused enough, you could actually be poisoned and still be all right. But up to now, the strength of your belief is not enough for that. But it is possible, and there are one or two on your planet who have proven this. If you want to know the condition of your mind in the past, examine your body now. If you want to know what your body will look like in the future, examine your mind now.

Q. Are we due another prophet?

A. How many would you like?

Q. Well, enough to bring us all together.

A. There are so many already. Is anybody listening?

LIFE-SUPPORT SYSTEMS - SPACESHIPS

Q. What exactly are UFOs or spaceships? Are they figments of our imagination?

A. The best I can do to explain from my own personal experience is to give the example demonstrated to me by spirit guidance.

(Shirley channeling) I am breaking through to a higher level. It is building up, and it takes a little while. I am told I have to explain this for the benefit of others who try the same. It is like the force of gravity, the g-factor when you go up in a rocket. I am feeling the pull, I feel as if I am going up with that pull. It is very weird and is not something I would have volunteered for in normal circumstances.

I can see flat, I can only call them platelets as it is the word I have got. Platelets, interlinking with each other. They are large and interlink rather as would your jigsaw puzzles, they are forming a complete platform.

"It is a support system. One that can be dismantled, manoeuvred, added to, and parts replaced. It is very adjustable, is it not? It is not as plain as it appears to the eye. Within the body of what you termed platelets, within this body invisible to the eye unless you have access, are many complicated structures of administration, circuits of administration system. It is self-motivating, self-replenishing, and self-repairing and constructed in such a manner as to be independent. It is dependent according to the will of those who manage these systems. I feel you ask what is this all for? As we have said, it is a support system, just one of many, and I feel your next question. Support for what? We will enlarge upon the subject, have no fear.

"There are many such platforms not only surrounding your planet but also surrounding your universe. There are many such—we will call them life-support systems from now on. There are many in existence in all universes for purposes of intermingling and traveling. Not only from one zone to another in a manner relating to physics but also in a manner relating to dimensions of time. Each one has a purpose and is manufactured for that specific purpose. We transmute from one system to another frequently according to changing needs.

"For example, should a group of our engineers require or feel the need to visit a certain zone, they may do so using one of these platforms, but not in a physical sense for it would take too long. We use our method of immediate transfer that can take place according to the combined will and procedures to be adopted. We can just as swiftly return to our starting point. It takes but a fraction of what you term time.

"Time in your sense is not real to us, and we have difficulty adapting to an existence that is bound by an organized system of events, one preceding another and events yet to be. We have great difficulty in adapting our procedure to be in line with the processes of your mechanisms. When the need arises for physical interaction and changing dimensions, we convert our platform or use another such as is available, which is purpose made for that need. It has equipment installed that may respond. These platforms are able to traverse time.

"If you were to be given the procedure, it would be meaningless to your most advanced physicists. This technology has been achieved by beings whose mind power and thought processes are fully utilized. We are able upon certain designated platforms to bring ourselves into recognition by the mortal being. There have been many times when this has been necessary. We have made use of your physical senses of sight, sound, feeling, and touch and all the other conscious senses.

"Access is available to you. It is a matter of adjusting. We are aware that attempts are being made at this time. We feel drawn to explain further upon our platforms. When your eyes—both inner and outer—are adjusted, they will become more visible to you when we wish it to be so. They have a purpose; you may term them as ships waiting offshore for evacuation when a volcano erupts. Do not take this literally please, it is an illustration only.

"Think upon the words *life-support system*. We have used these words quite deliberately to make it clear that we are engaged in securing the continuation of life-form as a breathing physical existence. We ensure the continuation of species. This is in order that we may utilize the assets that are available to us upon your planet that is considered to be an extraordinary place for habitation, one we do not wish to see eliminated in any way. We have come to your aid in times past, though you have not been aware.

"We are here to help those upon the surface of this extraordinary planet who are at present assisting us. It is upon these that we depend, and it is upon us that they depend. We work in union. There are platforms of a different notion whose ideas of conservation are a little at variance with ours. This matter is to be settled as it has importance."

ARE WE ALONE?

INTERPLANETARY VISITORS

Q. It would be nice to have an answer to the following question: Are there other life-forms in the universe, and what would they be like, how far away from us are they etc.?

A. According to space researchers, there are well over four hundred planets capable of intelligent civilizations within our own universe. It has been said that there are four hundred thousand races of various intelligences in space. Some of the well-known ones are the Hathors who are said to be the most advanced beings in the solar system and stand at fifteen feet tall. They operate from Venus in the fourth and fifth dimension.

Q. Are there extraterrestrials living on and visiting our Earth?

A. Tall white race of beings emerging.

The energy in my head was building and building to the enormous levels we have had before. Again, I wasn't sure if I could hold it. I had a picture of long thin white beings. Very long and spindly.

Shirley: I am seeing a different race of beings. Tall, white-skinned. Long and thin. They have been on Earth for oh so long.

"You haven't seen them simply because they are of a different dimension. Rather like your ghost figures. However, these are not ghost figures but simply a human race, similar in a sense to you but of a different dimension, existing on Earth at the same time as you. They are now emerging with the shift taking place in individuals and groups. With the shift taking place on all levels on the Earth, these long forms shall be seen. We are not to be confused with extraterrestrials for we are of the Earth. We have evolved beyond your present time but exist also in your time. Does that make sense to you?"

Note: the change between *we* and *they*, I feel, is due to both minds operating in mine. The division is not always clear-cut.

Q. Were you around in Atlantis times?

A. "We have been here long before Atlantis. We have come and gone. We had left—mmm! We haven't exactly died. We left Earth for a space of time and then decided to return. Being of a different dimension, we can do this without going through your physical incarnation cycle. The question, Were we around at a certain time? is a little difficult for us. We exist.

"We are real. We are more real than your incarnated third dimension. Because you have been unable to see us, to you we have not existed. It is simply a question of perspective, one that would intrigue your scientists to no end.
"We have evolved—it is difficult to say we have evolved differently. We observe your reality. It is to be hoped that you join in our reality when you leave your third dimension. We are not affected by cataclysmic events on your planet, for physical events do not damage us in the same way. However, we are not immune to emotions and mentality of the beings on this planet, those who jar our vibrations slightly. You can understand there is a slight ripple effect in the world of dimensional waves. All is connected, you see, even through one dimension to another. We keep in contact with many of your spiritual leaders."

Q. If people were to see or feel you, would they think of you as guardians or saviors?

A. "How others see us depends on each individual perspective. Some of complete unawareness of thought would think we were ghosts. Others who are rather more aware might consider us to be extraterrestrials, and others—it depends on perspective and background of belief. Others might consider us to be saints or etheric beings. We are after all, to some degree, etheric beings. How we are viewed would depend on the mentality and the soul's progression. It would not be the same for all.

We cannot say whether we would be regarded as saviors, though many might see us that way. Others might be afraid of us, which is why we have not been seen so much. My instrument here has seen us, though she does not remember the event."

Q. Are there many of you around?

A. "Oh yes. We are grouped in large numbers, we are not scattered thinly. So if you see one, you are sure to see many. We are not thin upon the ground."

Q. Are you in any particular places on the Earth?

A. "It is an interesting question. For we view the Earth differently to you. We do not view it with what is a good place to be in a geographic or climatic sense. We would be grouped where there is a purity of thought, where we feel comfortable with the emissions, the vibrations, irrespective of climatic conditions. There are certain areas on the globe that we enjoy. This might be on the equator. You might call them hot spots of energy. We group where the energies are good for us. It is difficult for us to be precise. There are many pyramids within your earth. There are pyramids in your oceans. We tend to group around the pyramids that are unsullied.

"We do attend and assist where there have been disasters, so then we leave our comfort zone and go to assist those who need us. We are not bound to one spot and can travel around. It is hard for us to prove any of this to you. If you were to see us *now* this evening, you would be hard put to describe our clothing or the color of our eyes. You would be hard put to find the detail in us. Drawing closer to our vibration, you might find you can describe the detail, and we would be delighted if you were to do so.

"We find it amusing at times when there is so much focus on maintaining your bodily strength. Whilst in physical form, you feel there is much advantage in this so that you do not suffer this or that illness. When you reach a point when you will know that it is your spirit and how you are emotionally and mentally that the body will take care of itself. You will not need to be concerned as to what you do and eat, whether you exercise this or that part of yourself. We have learned that all we need do is attend to the quality of our souls. This is why we do not appear to have a solid body. Rather long and lengthy. It has served us quite well.

"Are you able to see us yet? We do not have any hair. Our skin is what you would call translucent. We have long since dispensed with hair, that being closer to the animal form. We use our mind and our emotions to good effect. We also place our fingers on the human form to bring about a healing at times. We find it very hard to remain still, in one place. We feel we are in movement similar to plant life in your oceans. We wave with the current.

"All we have done by coming to you this evening is to give you another aspect of the realities of existence that are much broader than you might imagine. These are avenues for you to explore, to travel to in your unconscious state. So much to explore!"

Shirley: I feel a gentle smile. He has such a loving energy. I see clear blue eyes. Wonderful eyes!

Q. Will we finally meet beings from other planets, as in everyone seeing them and hearing them?

A. Yes. There are those called the Tall Whites that have been interacted with and that have a societal community complete with families, teachers, doctors, etc. They come and go as they please and have been doing so for some considerable time. (Read Charles James Hall's book *Millennial Hospitality*.) I personally have also been in contact with these particular visitors. There are many other types of space visitors on Earth. Some have been here before us. Some with humanlike appearances are living undetected among our society with no problem. You may have met them!

Q. Will everyone see flying saucers in the near future or just one or two people?

A. They are not all saucers of course. But yes, there will be masses of them. It will be undeniable that they are here. This won't please everybody, particularly those who are convinced by the biblical account as to how we began. This will throw a spanner in the works. According to religion, the beginning of man was Adam and Eve. If there is evidence of other beings that are not from Adam and Eve, then how does that sit with them? It would be uncomfortable to them as it throws their belief out of kilter. It is similar to those who were convinced the Earth was flat. Those who believed otherwise were imprisoned.

Q. Why is mankind in general so fearful of aliens? Is this due to humans having some negative group memory of visits in the past?

A. Fear of something unknown is common among humans. This has been used by governmental bodies to create false abductions and horror stories of ET and by the film industry with sensational films with horror stories of aliens. Aliens have traditionally been shown as something to fear. We do not like the very word *alien*."

Q. I hear of other sentient creatures scattered throughout our galaxy, and would like to ask if it is Earth's destiny to one day be incorporated into any extraterrestrial organizations, and if so, when might this happen?

A. As soon as we are considered to be spiritually responsible, we will join the galactic family.

Q. Will earthlings one day be able to travel to other star systems *in the physical plane,* or is that only available from the upper realms?

A. It is already possible to travel to other star systems and be there physically. There is a process of dematerialization and rematerialization. One day when we are included in the Galactic Federation, certain of us will be able to do this.

COSMIC BODY

Q. Is there a new planet coming toward Earth?

A. "Yes, it is indeed coming toward Earth. It is indeed coming, and it will leave."

Q. What is its name?

A. "Many names have been given to it. It is not important. It is very akin to your Earth. It will be close. It will not crash but will cause disruption.

It has been given various names by man as Vulcan, Nibiru, planet X, and so on."

It is said that from May 2011, it may be seen with the naked eye. By December 21, it may be seen as a second sun.

Q. Does it have a purpose?

A. "It is not exactly a deliberate purpose but a question of orbit. An orbit does not have a purpose, it just is. What you are asking is, 'Do the inhabitants have a purpose?' They do have a purpose of course."

Q. Will we see them?

A. "That is an unknown factor, but the feeling is yes, you will. The unknown factor is whether their presence is denied or accepted. It is known that minds on Earth do not see what they do not wish to see. It is common knowledge that they are very good at ignoring things."

Q. When will this be?

A. "The indication is for 2012. You are well aware that nothing is set. Although this orbit is due to be in place, there are **other factors** that sometimes deflect orbits. One of your giant planets in your solar system may deflect it slightly, so the timing and actual event is not set exactly. We feel we are hedging our answers here. Often when we say something categorically, we are held to account for misrepresentation, and we do not wish this to occur.

"We do our best with the knowledge that we have, and as you do, we too go by historical events. We too work out the system according to past occurrences. We do not intentionally misrepresent, but it can be seen as such, and then there is much laughter."

Q. Will it have an effect on our emotions and physicality?

A. "It will affect both of course. Emotions affect you physically. Gravitational effects will occur as will climatic changes. Of course there will be effects on all manner of things. Remember that life is eternal."

News fact: University of Washington astronomer Andrew Becker, who led the research team said, "**A newly discovered 'minor planet'** with an elongated orbit around the Sun may help explain the origin of comets." Researchers said on Monday the orbit of 2006 SQ372 is an ellipse four times longer than it is wide.

Q. But why can't we get even partial truths about this picture of reality . . . about ETs and planets? Someone, the media or government or someone else, is keeping this information from us.

A. "It is up to you to get those answers. Why do you watch six hours of television every day? Why do you feed your minds exclusively with the opinions of others? Why do you trust your politicians? Why do you trust your governments? Why do you support the destruction of your ecosystems and the companies and governments that perpetrate this destruction? You see, because the whole of humanity allows these things to occur, the wool is pulled over your eyes, and it's easy to ration information and direct your attention to mundane affairs like the weather and film stars. Is anybody interested enough to find out?"

DICLOSURE OF INFORMATION TO PUBLIC

Q. Will we be guided in disclosing the information you have just given in a palatable way to our fellow creation?

A. "We know that disclosure of the nature of this information will not come as a surprise to many. We are broadcasting through channelers and those who are receptive in many areas and in many languages. This is happening even where you would not expect them to have this knowledge because of remoteness. We note that you rely on technology for broadcasting in whatever way the information we have given you. This is not possible in all lands.

"So information is broadcast by other means and is just as effective. Do not be concerned about the content being nonpalatable. It is to reach the minds at all stages of development of mind and intellect. You have intellectuals among you on your planet who will look for the more technological aspects and will rely heavily upon scientific facts and data and will find proof."

CHAPTER 10

OUR FUTURE—2012

Q. What other predictions have there been?

A. Below are some descriptions of what has been given through trance work. Remember, these events are not set in stone and can be changed. They are simply possible futures. The dates tell when the predictions were given. Some of them have already come to pass.

MOVEMENT OF PEOPLES - August 21, 1991

I am in the Hall of Knowledge in the altered state and describe what follows.

"I see a tall ship, it is packed. It's on a stormy sea at night. It is packed with people from the black countries, black skins. They are looking to the west. They will come across stormy waters to settle and remain in the lands of their discovery. It's their new world of discovery. They will prosper. They will bring music and color. They will be many. They will grow and cultivate. They will cultivate the fields as in their former lands using the same methods, living the same lives, singing the same songs. They will teach their ways, it is a reversal of the past."

For me, it is like a television screen; the pictures start there and become real. It is strange; it is like watching a big video that you enter into and become a part of.

CHINESE PREDICTION - August 21, 1991

"The Chinese are highly evolved. They do not need to leave their lands. They will be invited to assist, to advise those outside their lands. They will be esteemed, they will give their counsel when *they* so desire, when they wish to do so. They feel self-sufficient and spurn the activities of the outside world. They are a world unto themselves.

"Their numbers will diminish in ways not related to birth control. It will be a blessing, a salvation. Even the people will see it as a salvation. It will be their strength. The intelligence will flourish like a flower. The wisdom will be ever present. The warlike emotions, aggressiveness will not be present, will not be necessary. They have no need (for aggression), no reason, nothing to gain, and everything to lose. Their wisdom will be admired and respected and sought after. They will be honored as peers."

AMERICA - PREDICTION - August 21, 1991

"There will be strong violent winds, storms across the prairies, in the towns. Violent! Yellow stormy skies, waves on the shore, high waves, high winds. It is a scene of natural calamity along the coastal areas. It is not (globally) catastrophic, it is humbling, and is a humbling levelling action. It is not disaster on a grand scale but a disaster for many.

"It is not important. The land and the people will survive and continue with a renewed set of values. It will be beneficial experience, but the storms will rage beforehand. Storms, snow (I can see snow) out of season. People will run to the mountains, but the mountains will rock. It will all settle, it will become quiet once more, reestablish. There will be a new pioneering spirit form afresh in the hearts of brave and strong peoples. They are survivors against adversity; it is a strengthening of souls that had become flaccid and wayward. It is a salvation of souls. There will be born geniuses in that time, men of special talents, men of clear sight."

And later on, I received this.

"The winds in America will blow more strongly than ever before. They are used to strong winds, but these will surpass anything previously experienced."

Possible choice of habitation

During one session, I saw that there would be choices as to how to live depending on the prevailing environment. One choice was to live under domes, vast areas undercover. I was reminded of the Eden Project in Cornwall. Another choice was to live under the sea. There would be long tunnels leading to undersea cities. I believe something like this already exists, but is secret.

SEPTEMBER 10, 1992
The Moon's Eyes

I have a picture of the moon and of man standing on the moon and the weightlessness and the dust and the craters that are seen as eyes. It's strange because I am looking at these crater eyes with the movement of the dust, when the eyes open like doorways, circular shuttered doorways with the shutters acting as eyelids. As they open, one can go in to the interior. That is strange, isn't it? (I wonder if this is related to the suggestions that there are bases on the moon?)

NB: I have a recording of a BBC radio 2 interview stating the existence of domes on the moon.

JUNE 7, 1992
INDUSTRIALIZATION TAKEN TOO FAR

I can see in my mind's eye an expanse of industry, factories, smoke. It's an industrial scene. As I look, there is a great big wave, as high as it can go. It is rolling across as a wave of red, a wall of red that is sweeping across the land. Like pulling a shutter of red across the scene, it is covering everything as it goes. The industrial scene can no longer be viewed through it anymore. The wave of red right way across has the quality of infrared, not a solid bright red. You almost feel you can see through it, but it is so difficult that one gives up the struggle to do so. It is as if you know behind it there is something there, but you cannot quite reach visually.

Out of this gloomy red step human beings. In twos at first, holding hands, an older and younger. As I watch and try to pin recognition on them, other humans are stepping out of the red silently, holding hands, in twos. Just stepping out of the gloom. Many are following and stepping out of this that has descended upon them. It is a strange thing to describe, and I cannot identify, but just know they are human beings stepping forward and surviving what has overtaken them. They are silent, no words, just two by two, not a great horde. Slowly but with a sense of bewilderment, with a sense of coming out of dreamtime and not really fully aware of what has happened. Dazed and recovering but with a sense of bewilderment and shock about them. They have survived.

I asked what period of time this was.

"It is when your industrialization has reached the pitch where it cannot be contained any longer. When it reaches explosion point and cannot be encompassed within the law of things. That is when this scene will take place."

I see mountains like the Alps with water almost up to the peaks. As I watch, the water freezes so that it is solid from the ground up, i.e., down to the ground.

JUNE 11, 1992
MOVEMENT OF POPULATIONS

I have a picture of dwarflike people, eyes that look at you as if every thought is known to them, telepathic. Now it changes, and there is a picture of people skating over ice, smooth ice like a frozen lake. There is no danger for the ice is solid down to the ground. This is ice on land. I'm shown what appear to be caves on hillsides, and there are people sheltering, huddled and trying to keep warm in the caves. I don't know if they really are caves. They're huddling close to each other, groups of people looking out at the frozen land.

They look bewildered as if they don't know what has happened. The sky is very dark, and it has a green tinge, a very unusual color. It is not a natural color. They have no provisions and have nothing but themselves. I don't know how they can help themselves. They must venture out and search, for they must not stay where they are. They will not survive if they stay where they are. I have a strong feeling that this has happened in the past, it has already happened before. There must be movement of peoples. That is what they are trying to say.

"There must be movement; one cannot remain in the same lands if there is to be survival. It is useless to cling to the homeland. Large scale movement of population to areas of growth is essential."

As if to show an example, I am given a picture of people who live at the foot of a volcano, and whenever it erupts, they rebuild later in the same place. In this case of the caves shown it would be stupidity, they must move.

JUNE 23, 1992
NEW THINKING RESTRUCTURE

I have a picture of men tearing up papers and substituting others in their place. I can't quite work that one out.

"The papers are documents relating to scientific research. Figures, calculations, and formulae long established will be replaced. A new thinking, a new direction of endeavour is required. The old conditioning will be swept aside. Restructure, there is to be restructure (of energies?)"

I can't understand.

"Restructure of both on a material and physical level. Genetically speaking, there is to be restructure. One might say rapid evolution. Yes, indeed there will be changes that you cannot imagine."

I ask for a picture. I know it sounds absolutely crazy, but it is not the first time that I have had it, so don't laugh, will you? It's a picture of people in the air without any visible means of support. Oh, it is clear.

"It is a demonstration of ability to defy gravity, antigravity you might say. It is not necessary to escape the pull of your earth to experience this and to utilize this in many ways for transport and other objectives useful to mankind. It has in fact been done before; this has been achieved in your past but was misused. It will be so again."

MAY 28, 1992
GLOBAL CHANGE AND OTHER WORLDS

Somebody said, "We have got lift off." I see a big television set, but it is a panoramic view like a viewing point, like a television screen without a boundary. All I can see at the moment is a sea with a big swell on it, rolling. I can feel the motion. I can see the sea, and underneath the water, I can see as well. It is like a cut-out view. Under the sea are mountains; I can see mountains below the water. As I watch, the water is stilled, frozen, a dead stillness.

A guide sitting with me and watching says, "Everybody thinks of the warming as being a rising of temperature. Consequences are not always so, the consequences alter patterns to the extent that there is a dramatic lowering of temperature not previously imagined in certain areas. A shift in position of temperate zones. Siberia one imagines as being the area of intense cold. That is a mistake; there will be a reversal. Those now wishing to be anywhere but in Siberia will gladly remain there, a land of plenty, of abundance, of pleasurable existence."

I see a land peopled by many; they are short people, very short. I see vast canopies, enormous expanse, enormous expanse of covering, manmade artificial covering over the land. I don't know if this is here or on another planet.

"It is a means of existence elsewhere, perfectly practical and feasible; one that may need to be created for the continuance of life in certain areas. Environment!"

Talk about science fiction!

"What is fantasy to you is quite normal for those who live in this manner. Your method of existence to the eyes of many appears to them to be fantasy, a world in the imagination only. We who have communication and knowledge know and fully realize that there are many facets to life, as you yourselves are aware that thought alone is also an existence. There are many (worlds) that even you would find difficult to comprehend."

He is showing me squares and triangles and shapes in colors, and they are all moving about—everything is a shape of geometric form.

"That too is a reality every bit as valid as your own."

At this moment, a different tone of voice came in.

"Note when the birds fly in. The birds know. The birds will take to the air in numbers and are directed. They have a sense of purpose and know their direction. When the birds take to the air, that is the time. That is the time for more than just communication. They will take to the air in numbers great. It will be noticed. That is when you should be aware of something to happen of relevance to the discussion. You will also notice an attempt to take to the air those birds that have lost the power of flight. The urge will be to take flight once more, even though it is physically impossible. This too will be noted. It is a primeval instinct that will surge once again. It will be so strong as to override reason. What we are saying is that logic will take flight."

It is difficult to receive this clearly. He is giving me a picture because I can't find the words. There is somebody holding my thumbs. I will describe. All the flightless birds are struggling hard to fly, and they can't. I feel this may be symbolic.

JANUARY 13, 1993
WATERS FLOODING COUNTRY TO COUNTRY

I am being shown something, a picture of icy waters pouring from one land to the other. Waters pouring from one country to the other, flooding, not directed. Pouring, flowing, and carrying with it mud. All is washed away in the flood. Mud, animals, objects all washing along in the tide. I am asking where this is.

"In many lands not just one, not just one continent. In many over the same period. Waters on the eastern sides; rivers rising and flowing backward. Some will welcome the water, indeed to many it will be a salvation. It will be a renewal, hope that will spring again and cries of halleluiah. Waters will deflect the attention that is resting so heavy at this time. An order of priorities will be reestablished. They will not be as now; it will not be man against man. It will be man with man."

FEBRUARY 27, 1993
PRIMEVAL SWAMPS

I have someone with a silver head. He has eagle eyes, and the nose is like a beak. It is right in front of me, so strong. The eyes are looking so unblinking into mine; it is a joining of eyes. I can feel being pulled toward them. Into each eye, there is a picture like looking into a television screen. There is a lot of dust, swirling dust. One might almost say a dust storm, dry, barren, and dry hot winds; the sun is red, deep red. I have never seen the sun that red, as if it's not the sun. Enormous, it is very hot and over the surface of the ground there are creatures, close to the ground like lizards. They are adapted to the heat.

"It is not everywhere." This came in answer to my unspoken question.

He flipped a coin, and the other side is steam, wet. They are not merging, they are distinct. I don't understand any of this! There are no seas, no ocean.

"This is a temporary phase. It is not so long."

There are birds, I have just seen birds. I keep getting the feeling that it might not be our future. Perhaps that is just wishful thinking. It is the red sun that is puzzling me. Now I understand.

"It is what has been, but what was can return."

Thinking about the seas I got the words *primeval swamps*. I don't know why they are doing this. They are emphasising a point of being and Creation.

"We are putting things in perspective. You (mankind) have lost your sense of perspective in the overall pattern. You are too wrapped up in minor events. The perspective will make your existence much more understandable. It will produce a calmness and serenity and direction for each. If only the perspective of the whole was held in sight there would be no need to kill, to envy, to seek after other's possessions. It would put things in balance."

It is the man who is talking who is also the eagle. The pictures have gone. He is the person with the long nose. He is like a magician as he keeps changing.

"We can use whatever means that will penetrate your mentality."

MARCH 12, 1993
FLOODS IN DESERT

As I lie on the sand, all sorts of creatures are coming up to sniff at me. There's a snake, not at all frightened of me; there's a little small fox. I am an object of investigation and interest. I lie quite still so as not to disturb them. There are all sorts of little creatures here. A falcon comes and perches on my hand.

There is tremendous lightning in the sky. A storm, it's raining heavily, really torrential. It's raining on the desert in sheets without ceasing. The downpour goes on and on until water begins to form in the hollows, which creates even deeper recesses. The rain pours off the rocks in high places. When the time passes the water that flows over these rocks forms a lake in the depth below until the lake grows and rivers flow from the lake, permanent. The birds rejoice and come to drink and drop their seeds and the greenery returns. It provides nesting and life returns. I get a picture of a waterfall, the rain keeps on coming.

MAY 7, 1993
PREDICTION OF MUSLIM-INVOLVED WAR AND NEW LANDS EMERGING

"You must record this."

The Arabs, the Muslims in the Arab states will involve themselves in the war at present in the Yugoslav areas. They will involve all countries where there are Muslims in numbers sufficient to unite. It will become a matter of pride and furthering belief in one's system. Politically motivated but driven by the feeling raised up in the peoples. Turkey will be involved as will surrounding nations, and the funding will come from the Muslim states, in particular the Arabs. This is for the record."

They are still with this.

"There is pestilence and contamination from sources out of Russia, contamination that will cause many to fall sick. The contamination will hit all sides irrespective of religion or race. It is when the winds blow strong from the East, when the wind is steady from the East. There is much wailing, much lamenting. Such a cry as has never been heard before."

I am trying to pin it down. (I hope this will not be another Chernobyl.)

And later during the same evening's session, more came:

"There are waters rolling over the land from the North. From the Northern extremities the waters will come."

They are showing me a picture of the water rolling gently, not a tidal wave.

"The waters rolling gently down and barely noticeable but inexorable and unstoppable. The waters will come from the North. There will be new lands; new fertile lands that were not in sight before. They will be a blessing when the time is needy. Virgin land, untainted, not plundered and rich in soil. There will be a period after the emergence of these lands of biting insects. This will be a feast for the creatures of the air that will grow fat and prosper. When the balance has been set this land will be fit for habitation.

"It is a period spread over time and is not sudden, but is a slow growth. These things are given to you, to give you hope during moments and long periods that we have laid out for you. It is not all a picture of despair and disaster. There will be in the final outcome of this stage a beneficial effect. Although it will feel lengthy and you will feel there is no end to the misfortunes of man, the dark period will not last forever and the light will come again."

JUNE 4, 1993
MAN'S CONSTRUCTION - WIND OF CHANGE

I have a picture of a tower block. It is reaching up high so that the top of the building is in the clouds. There are hands on all sides of the block holding it up. I don't understand the meaning of this except the hands and the arms are supporting the building. Not just one pair of hands but several supporting the building, the dwelling places. I ask for clarification.

"So that the world built up by man, built by man and constructed by man, so that this world does not crumble and fall killing all occupants of this constructed world, we are attempting to hold it in place. We are attempting to hold it together against the winds of change and the winds of force that buffet this construction. We are attempting to steady and retain in position until the winds have passed. It may be that our efforts will be in vain but we are attempting to do what we can.

"You cannot see the construction above the clouds. It is lost from your view but those who live in lofty places, those who have deemed it right for them to live in the higher echelons of your society, those who have decided that is their rightful position; they will not receive the same support for the simple reason we cannot see into the cloud. Those who rise and put themselves in the higher positions would have the furthest to fall if their construction collapses. Unless they are able to fly they would not survive the fall.

"We are doing what we can. We are talking of winds of change, winds that blow from a direction unknown to you, from a direction you have not dreamed of. You will not be prepared because your eyes are not turned in the direction from which the change will come. Those of you who have the sight to see, sight from within, will not place themselves in the dwelling places constructed by man's vanity. They will seek the open spaces and remain close to the ground from which they cannot fall. They will avoid the vanity of man's rise above others and above the creatures who cannot construct. Those men who have this foresight will not be crushed should the edifices crumble."

JUNE 25, 1993
PREPARATION FOR CHANGES

I have a picture now of a lot of aeroplanes flying over. They are dropping leaflets, lots and lots and lots of leaflets.

"They are going a long way and the cargo is full of these leaflets. They are printed in all languages, every language that exists. There can be no one who will say they were not told. There can be no avoiding the knowledge, even those who cannot read will understand. How each individual reacts is according to their own will, their own decision. There will be many who ignore and there will be many who take heed. The messages will be broadcast also through the airwaves, through the television."

I want to know what the message is.

Q. How long off is it?

A. "Protect, protect, cover—do not run. You can conserve, disconnect—
disconnect all amenities, all sources of supply—(I am getting very hot)
protection.

There is a wall so high—it is water. I can't stay with that one. It was
getting so uncomfortable and was as if I was physically there within that
scene. A tidal wave I feel is referred to. Note: Since then in 2005, there have
been tsunamis in Indonesia.

JULY 2, 1993
BIRD MESSENGERS ARE VITAL

I have a picture of a lot of birds flying over the ocean.
"They are flying from one land to the other carrying grain. They
are not only the messengers but also the bringers of new life. They will
avoid the upheavals and will endure and be responsible for the seeding
of the Earth. They are messengers, providers for the continuation of life.
Do not poison the birds of the air for they are vital for your comfort.
They are vital for the destruction of biting stinging insects that will
torment.
"You have need of the birds; you have need of as many birds as can be
found. There cannot be too many if you are to keep the balance of comfort
for humanity. Changes will produce insects on a grand scale. Pay attention
to that which you put upon your soil."
They are giving me a picture of horses and cattle and various animals all
trying to get at the insects that are troubling them. They are not showing
people but animals. I think it is just to make a point. He is nodding as if to
say yes. It is a strange one this evening. A show!

JULY 9, 1993
TURKEY (prediction)

I have another picture. You know little fluffy chicks when they are newly
hatched? I have loads of these little chickens.
Sitter: They are turkeys.
Are they? I wouldn't know a chicken from a turkey at this stage. I am
waiting for them to tell me what this is about.

"Turkeys make a lot of nonsensical noise and that is exactly what is going on within the boundaries of Turkey. The events taking place are at the stage of squabbling, but the squabbling will develop into more serious irritation and anger when the biggest birds and the strongest will peck at the weaker ones and there is fighting one with another, brother against brother. The strongest will prevail at the expense of the smaller and less able. What appears to be innocent, even delightful grows into something more sinister and disagreeable."

I am getting the feeling to pay attention.

"Not that there is anything that you can do but to be aware. Do not be taken by surprise. Not to gloss over events as insignificant for it is the insignificant events that will become the most important. So insignificant that they may be missed, except if you have a sharp eye and a quick ear. You wouldn't want us to give you the whole story, would you?"

NEW ZEALAND

I was in New Zealand in 1999 and was staying on the island of Waiheke. While there I was looking out to sea at all the other islands. Suddenly I saw that the water had vanished. I could see bare ground where there had been sea. It was a shock, and I noticed that all the islands were bare of water. Then it was back to normal again. Was this a sign of a tsunami to come or a rising up of the land? Only time will tell.

During a later channeling, we received this.

"There will be movement, both of populations and of land mass. There will be strong winds. We know you have them already, but these winds will increase to levels that have not been reached before. There will be a rising of the waters. This you know already. This is already established by your scientists. We tell you that there will be mass movement of peoples. In itself, this should tell you that it will be a necessity not just a desire. Climates that have been cold will become warm. Land that has been desert will become seas.

"Man will survive. Man will always survive. The great landmasses such as the continents and the inner parts of continents will be the places that are the safest. But there will be strong winds nevertheless. Australia will be inhabited more fully than it is at the moment. There will be no restriction of entry into that country. Many of the small islands will become larger landmasses, for they will rise. There will be a change in the contours of land. There will be more water than previously. Mountains will fall.

"There will not be a comet strike. We tell you this for this is a question in the minds of your officials. There will not be an actual hit by an asteroid, which is what we meant to say. However there will be a gravitational pull as a result of asteroid. A gravitational shift as a result, without the strike. This is something to be grateful for. There will be—we try not to give doom and gloom. You see how we are struggling not to tell you all things. You have one on your planet, one volcanic interaction that is greater than you have ever had before. This will cause some disruption."

Q. Will December 21, 2012, go by as just another day, or will there be dramatic happenings?

A. I do not think anybody really knows, not even the celestial beings. Nothing is ever cast in stone and is flexible according to man's thinking and belief. Events are already underway, and there are important changes happening all the time. Some people notice these changes and many more do not. For those who are unaware, it may be just another day. There will be several millions of people who are not ready in their spiritual development or acceptance, and these ones will not see a change.

Q. The question that comes to my mind is what exactly is going to happen on the December 21, 2012? I understand a large cosmic body is approaching, but what does this have in store for our current way of life? Will life ever be the same again, or come January 2013, will we even notice a difference?

A. There have been many predictions regarding a cosmic body affecting planet Earth. For example. my own prediction in 1993:

I have a picture of roof tops at night and stars. It is quiet, and everybody is sleeping. I have another picture. It is a golden globe in the distance. It is rolling along toward us.

"It is beautiful but it is equally perilous. It has a force which is natural to it, a force it cannot help but have. This force has an effect upon the surroundings and such things as are in the vicinity of this force. It is a beauty and a wonder and at the same time something which is not welcome. It is the attraction, the attraction of the pull. A combining of forces that is not in all cases to the benefit of both forces. It is nonetheless a thing of beauty and to be wondered at as a marvel. It is a portent. It is an indication of the means by which change will come about upon your planet."

But even predictions are not set in stone and are often given simply to wake us up as to our soul's purpose.

Q. *Where should I move to?*

A. What is important is not where you live, but who you live with. This is to say a like-minded community is by far the safest place to be.

Q. Are we about to have a pole shift on Earth? If so will this end the human race?

A. The poles have shifted many times in our past, and magnetic north constantly moves. The human race survived those times, and it is expected that it will survive in the future.

Q. *I'm worried about 2012 and what is going to happen. It would appear that lots of people are going to die in catastrophes. Is this true do you think?*

A. To many this may sound ominous, but the beings of light have assured us that we are the creators of circumstance not victims of circumstance. We do not have to just stand by and wait for disaster to strike. A prophecy from on high that contains the potential of a negative or destructive outcome is given to humanity only if we have the ability to do something to avert that particular outcome. That is in fact, the *sole* reason why such a prophecy is given to humanity. (My thanks to the writer who gave this opinion.)

Any negative prediction is intended to show us the potential of what may occur based on known facts at the time of the prediction. The intention of such a prediction is to inform us and to inspire us to do something about it and alter the path we are following. As the alarm gets louder it is more difficult to hit snooze.

Q. If we have done our best to be light workers, do we stand more chance of survival? Some human religions believe that they are the only ones to be saved from an Armageddon type event.

A. Light workers in the main are here to serve others and if it is their decision to carry on being of help, then it is probable that they will survive in order to do so in times of difficulty for those who cannot help themselves. It will depend on the choices made before incarnating.

Q. Will there be events that will cause waves of lower vibrating people (or people who do not want to ascend with the current body), to transition before 2012, for example, through natural disasters of fire, earth, air, and water, pandemics, etc.

Q. It is said that people of lower vibrations (for example those who frequently act out of violence, or put the welfare of themselves before all others) will not be able to exist in the higher vibrations of the New Earth. Will their lives appear to terminate through natural means such as disease, accidents, wars or acts of violence?

A. "We shy away from passing any judgment on other souls. What we can say is that all souls carry a vibration that is comfortable for them to have. There are different vibration rates that hold energy. To be able to ascend to a higher rate, one must have a compatible level of energy that is comfortable for them. To give an analogy: If you put a weak current into a strong current it will be destroyed, blow a fuse so to speak. To put it another way, dark cannot be put into light without it being transformed into light or destroyed. Each soul through its journey will have assumed an energy or light that is comfortable.

"Since the transition you speak of requires a higher rate of light and energy only those who are comfortable with it will transit. Those who die through natural disasters or other means are not necessarily of lower vibrations. Some have already moved on to higher planes. Others intend to reincarnate back to the period of transit or just after. Many who are not ready for a change will die and eventually re-incarnate back onto a third-dimensional world to work out their own progression. Others who are spiritually responsible will work with the change and for the betterment of others, as you are doing now. It will be tough but while there is realization that life goes on—there is no end—it will be dealt with happily. A turnaround is inevitable."

A BETTER WORLD

I am seeing a picture. The sun is not in the same position. It has a different color. They have just shown me a band of people, a united band of people. They have each got a hand over the heart and the other hand joined to the one next to him.

"They are pledging themselves to a better world. It is a group of souls who are at present incarnated and those who are yet to be incarnated through choice, at a time when the planet needs just guidance. There are many, they have chosen to be in all diverse lands and will be in positions of influence and assistance to ensure the light begins brightly to give courage and strength and to set the pattern. This is their pledge that they are making."

Q. Are there pockets of light workers developing around the world to repopulate following the catastrophe?

A. "Yes, there are many who have been prepared and who have incarnated specifically to assist. Not everywhere is subject to catastrophe."

DIMENSIONS

Q. It is said that we are multidimensional. Will we learn how to be aware in different dimensions simultaneously?

A. That level of awareness is not for everybody for not all can cope with that experience, even as multidimensional beings. For the most part, it is possible to be aware of another dimension and to be focused on it without being confused. In time we will be able to manage more.

Q. If we shift to fifth density for a time in our daily lives, is this perceived as more of a blissful state or do we actually see different surroundings?

A. If seen from a third-dimensional reality then the fifth would appear to be much brighter. The surroundings would be as you might imagine them to be. You create the reality.

Q. If a third-density person were watching a light worker changing states to a fifth-dimensional state of consciousness, would the light worker disappear from the observer's view (ala the Celestine Prophecy).

A. This can and does happen and depends on the ability of the observer to see this. I have frequently disappeared from view while channeling and entering different states of being. This has happened even in broad daylight.

Q. If the New Earth after Ascension is the existing Earth only bathed now in the higher vibrations of the fifth dimension what will happen to all the twentieth and twenty-first century residues of civilization such as freeways, cities, shopping malls, etc? Will the New Earth citizens have to work to dismantle these—turning them back to nature or replaced with a more refined architecture suitable as a fifth-dimensional expression?

A. All dimensions exist at the same time in their different states of existence. Therefore the third-dimensional earth will still exist as it is now complete with freeways etc and only be affected by the physical changes due to occur over the coming years. What you term the New Earth in the fifth dimension will have what it always has had in that progression of time.

To make it clearer, if the old Earth, i.e. third-dimensional earth were to no longer be, how is it that guides, spiritual teachers and visitors from the higher dimension still have contact with us? Jesus came from a higher state and yet he incarnated back to our third dimension from his, both dimensions existing at the same time.

> Time is not at all what it seems. It does not flow in only one
> direction, and the future exists simultaneously with the past.
> Albert Einstein

SCIENTIFIC KNOWLEDGE

Scientific knowledge indicates that there will be climatic and geographical changes in our future time on Earth which may well be catastrophic. What they can't tell us is when. It has happened in the past and still the human race has continued as it will in the future.

Information given by respected scientist Mitch Battros: **Producer - Earth Changes Media -Author:** *'Solar Rain - The Earth Changes Have Begun'*

The perpetrators are streams of charged particles blasting off the Sun in what is known as the solar wind. Researchers were stunned to discover recently that Earth is losing more of its atmosphere than Venus and Mars, which have negligible magnetic fields.

Solar Cycle 24 has begun—and it has been predicted by NASA, NOAA and ESA to be up to 50 percent stronger than its 'record breaking' predecessor Cycle 23 which produced the largest solar flare ever recorded. The Sun will reach its 'apex' (maximum) in late 2011 into 2012.

"I believe it will be the magnetic influence produced by the Sun which will usher in what is described by our ancient ancestors as "the transition" bringing us to a new state-of-being". Just as the Sun's solar activity affects the Earth's magnetic field which has a dramatic affect on Earth's "weather" i.e. earthquakes, floods, volcanoes, hurricanes; so does this wave of electrical currents affect the human body's magnetic field. Mitch also reveals a little-known development from modern medicine known as Transcranial Magnetic Stimulation (TMS). TMS provides empirical evidence of how magnetic fields can influence human emotions. **Mitch Battros**

STARGATES

Q. I have heard of a star gate opening at this time. If so can the details and significance of this happening be explained? How often do 'star gates' open on or around the earth?

A. It has been posited that a Parallel Earth time line will meet our Earth's time line in 2012 and we will be able to cross over as in Star gates. I don't know how true this is. There are many Star gates all over the Earth and they do not all open at the same time. Many are hidden. This is a subject for another book.

MESSAGE FROM THE FUTURE

Each individual act is important to the health of your world.

Planet Earth will survive. The human species will survive. During channeling sessions from time to time we are having quite clear strong visits from one who states he is from our far future. This is not imagination since all who were present feel that very special energy and were aware of this being, so tangible it could almost be touched. This says to us that we do have a future, one that is bright. The message that follows is clear.

"We are going to talk about the future for we feel this is in your mind and you wish to know what you could do. How can you best serve? Where should you be? What should you do? Your soul is important, your soul as a grouping, as a species of mankind will continue. There will be changes; there have always been changes so this is not new. We feel that your own personal focus is more on the near future rather than the far future. You are all so very concerned about your future, which is quite understandable, but do you realize that your future stretches into infinity? Focus on your present, for as you think and act today will dictate your tomorrow.

"So is it not important to think about what you are feeding your mind with? Are you feeding your mind with scenes of violence, negative thoughts and ignoble acts? Or are you filling your mind with the glories of being alive in your wonderful world, and with stories of acts of brave and heroic individuals and the amazing work done by light workers? Be inspired by the astounding examples of those who give of their time, love and compassion to those less fortunate than themselves. Your mind will absorb all the food you give it and this in itself will affect your future.

"There is a future, yes. There are many possible futures and not all are the same. Much of what we say you already know. Many of you are going to say: 'Well we know this stuff'. However at times you need reminding because it is easy to forget what you know. Well-meaning people say, 'you have it all within', and that irritates because you can't remember what you have within, is this not so? You see all you need do is reflect a little longer and not dash about quite as much as you do, filling all your moments with unimportant matters.

"What is important is how you feel about yourself. Do not do anything you would dislike yourself for. When you feel about yourself in a good way, then you are looking after your own soul development, your own soul growth. This is what is important, for this dictates your future.

"It is not important if you are on this planet or another planet, on a spaceship or on the Earth. What is important is how you feel about your own particular soul. Understand the concept that all is one, that everything is united in one great consciousness, and that you are as important as everybody else.

"So your future? And we can hear you say, well when are you going to tell us about the future? There are always changes. We make contingency plans to assist the planet Earth and much of this is an infusion of special souls. Many are being born now, many have already been born. These are highly developed souls who have volunteered to be of service when there is a need. **Are you one of these?** We are also speaking of interaction with the mind, supplying ideas and technology to assist, to keep civilization going.

"Realize that you have many practical people who know what they are doing on the planet. They know how to build a house, they know how to construct this or that or the other. These individuals who are alive today are vital for they will step forward and put things right. It is a bit like being marooned on a desert island and somebody comes up and says "Ah well, I can build a shelter because I know how to do it". There will be those who know how to heal without the use of medicine. These individuals will be there when there is a need to rebuild society; they will be there to help those who haven't got a clue how to do anything, who do not know how to wash their clothes unless they have a washing machine. They do not realize it yet but these special ones will always step forward and come to the aid of those who haven't got any idea. **Are you one of these?**

"Along with that you have special star beings who have volunteered to be human. Some of them have never been human before, but are now incarnated as human specifically to assist mankind to get back on its feet, whether this be spiritually or of a practical nature, or with health and healing. **Are you one of these?**

"Concentrate on your own life and your role for this planet, for you do have a role—those who are healers will heal, those who are teachers will teach, those who have serenity of mind will bring calm to those who are not serene, those who understand disturbed minds will be able to soothe them and arrange some method of assistance, those who are practical will put their practical gift to use, those who bring joy with music and dance and laughter will do so. Each has a role to play and each is as valuable as the other. You will have noticed that there are many young ones who are astounding in what they are able to do, and these numbers are increasing all the time.

"You have those such as from Arcturus, Sirius, Orion, and the Pleiades who are bringing forward ideas into the minds of those who are receptive enough to receive the ideas. **Are you one of these?** This is where your past developments have come from. People think it is some clever people who've thought of something new. Yes, it is, but the idea has been given to them from a star system, from a group of beings on a star system who are helping the technology and the development of your species with these ideas. Now it is up to you as an individual whether you recognize these gifts and accept them or whether you simply do not hear them. **Are you one of these?**

"Dreams, meditation, channeling, any means of contact with the spirit world is absolutely vital. Many are being trained now to connect with the spirit world. **Are you one of these?** It is not random; it is a program to enable people to make connection for themselves so that many more will be awake. The numbers will grow so that there will be enormous help through this means. Those who close their ears and do not wish to have anything to do with this will be assisted by those who do. **Are you one of these?**

"Is it always somebody else who must make things happen? Is it always somebody else's responsibility? If each individual took full responsibility for being the best they can be with what attributes they have, if each did this everywhere, then the whole of the planet would be transformed and healed in an instant and the job would be done.

"It is no accident that you have chosen to incarnate in this exciting time. Each of you here is going to make a difference. You are here to swing the balance to the desired outcome. We urge you; please dear souls, to think about your own role, no matter how to your mind, it appears to have no bearing on the greater work. We are aware that you know all the theories, you know the concepts, that you are connected, that you are all of one mind. But it still comes down to each individual.

"How can you know what your role is? What do you do? You may go to someone who will give you a reading, in the hope that they will tell you what your role is. Or you will meditate and ask of your guides what you are supposed to be doing, for you would do it if you only knew what it was. The first step is to ask yourself what you desire to do. Most of the fear that human beings have comes because they are concerned if there will be a change in their lifestyle, a change in events that will affect them personally. "Will I still have my job?" "What will we do if there is no oil?" Without seeing the bigger picture, they are worrying unnecessarily.

"To advance spiritually, conduct yourself according to spiritual laws and spiritual values. When you meet challenges, greet them with joy, for that is yet another gift that will help you to advance. When you endure pain with fortitude, this is yet another means of advancing you. When you surmount the trials as they arrive with the right attitude, when it does not beat you down but lifts you up, then you have advanced. When you look at another soul and genuinely feel love. You do not have to like all souls, but if you can love them as souls, then you are advancing yourself, for love will advance you. Now we do know it is not easy to love everybody, it is easy to be judgmental, for it comes unbidden when one sees a fault in another. But if you can try to see the one that you judged instantly in another light and refer to them in your mind as simply another soul learning their way, finding the path for themselves, then you will find love for the striving that is going on, or for the unhappiness that is within them, you will aim to release the pain, to ease the burden, rather than condemning."

"Never think that what you do in life makes no difference to your planet. Just keep in mind the 'Hundred Monkeys' syndrome. No matter how large or small you consider your contribution to be, rest assured that when you act with good intention you personally make a difference to the health of your own soul and well being of your planet and all its inhabitants. You are here right now to experience the greatest adventure of all time. Enjoy it."

QUESTIONS FROM SPIRIT TO YOU

These are intended for philosophical debate and were posed by our spiritual guides.

Q. When you climb a mountain, which is the best route to take? The zigzag path or the straight-up climb?

A. "I would like to ask if you sincerely believe that what you do in whatever way, is it of value? It is a question that you may ask yourselves. Do you have belief within you, or are you merely experimenting and hoping? Is the belief firm? When you find one that rings true to your heart, then that is the method for you, and I say method when I mean engagement in whatever activity you are engaged in. When you believe that your whole being, your intent, and your love is being utilized through the activity you have chosen, then you may know that it is effective. First you must believe; that is vital. That is a question for all who may wish to ask of themselves.

"We would also ask another question. What you engage yourselves in, ask yourselves why? Why do you do it? Do you busy yourselves with helping others in whatever activity for reasons of advancing your soul, for being of assistance to your sisters and brothers, or do you engage yourselves to see what you might learn and what you might discover and so be enlightened, or is it a sum of all those things? They are questions that are important to your development. The motivation has great importance. The reason for which one does something has a greater importance than the deeds or the effects.

"It is your motivation and what is in your heart that is counted. Do it with joy. Whatever you do, do it with happiness, and if you can find no happiness in your actions, then cease, cease them and look for one that gives you pleasure and joy. Life is not to be a penance, it is not to be a trial, it is to be fulfillment that should be joyous and happy and that joy and happiness will be felt by the recipients of your efforts. If you do not carry this happiness within you, then your recipients will receive whatever strain you are putting on yourself, the anxieties and perhaps despondences. So keep this too in mind, if you cannot feel happiness in what you do, then cease and look for an alternative. That is the best advice I can offer you. Whatever it is that you do, enjoy life and look to the future with optimism."

Do look out for my next book soon to be published titled *Being Human*.

News of this will be on my Web site: www.little-owl.org

Also not to be missed are the Little Owl Cards, now in their third printing and available through my Web site.

ACKNOWLEDGMENTS

My eternal thanks to all those who have supplied the questions and who sincerely wish for answers. Without you, this book would not exist.

My thanks to the spirit world for their response to those questions.

My thanks to my son David who has helped me through the tangle of computing and for his enormous patience and encouragement.

©2010 Shirley Humphreys Battie
35 Hood Crescent
Bournemouth
Dorset BH10 4DB
UK

Tel: (44) 01202 517557
Shirley@littleowl.force9.co.uk
www.little-owl.org

INDEX

A

abortions, 69. *See also* pregnancy
Abram, 104
accidents, 19, 36, 66, 91, 143, 149
Adam, 125
afterlife, 18, 67, 81-82. *See also* incarnation; reincarnation
Akashic Records, 92
aliens, 99, 126. *See also* extraterrestrials; UFO
amnesia, 39
animal souls, 23
Anthony, Saint, 105
apes, 99. *See also* evolution
Arabs, 136-37
Arcturus, 87, 149
Ariel, 100
Ascended Masters, 28, 44, 102
asteroid, 141
astral traveling, 36, 38-40, 44, 72, 95
Atlantis, 123
atoms, 42, 45, 64, 88
awakening, 17, 46, 65-66, 113, 116
ayahuasca, 111

B

beasts, 110
Becker, Andrew, 128
Bible, 33, 104. *See also* Christians
brain, 47-50, 109, 116
  exercises, 48
  See also mind

C

catastrophes, 142, 144
celestial sons, 99, 102. *See also* Ascended Masters; evolution; White Brotherhood
Celestine Prophecy, 145
chakras
  brow, 112
  crown, 112
  first, 111
  sacral, 111
channeler, 22, 27, 30, 41-45
channeling, 27, 30, 32, 41-44, 103, 140, 145, 147, 149
Charlatans, 20
Christians, 33

CPSIA information can be obtained at www.ICGtesting.com
Printed in the USA
LVOW050030200712

290778LV00002B/75/P